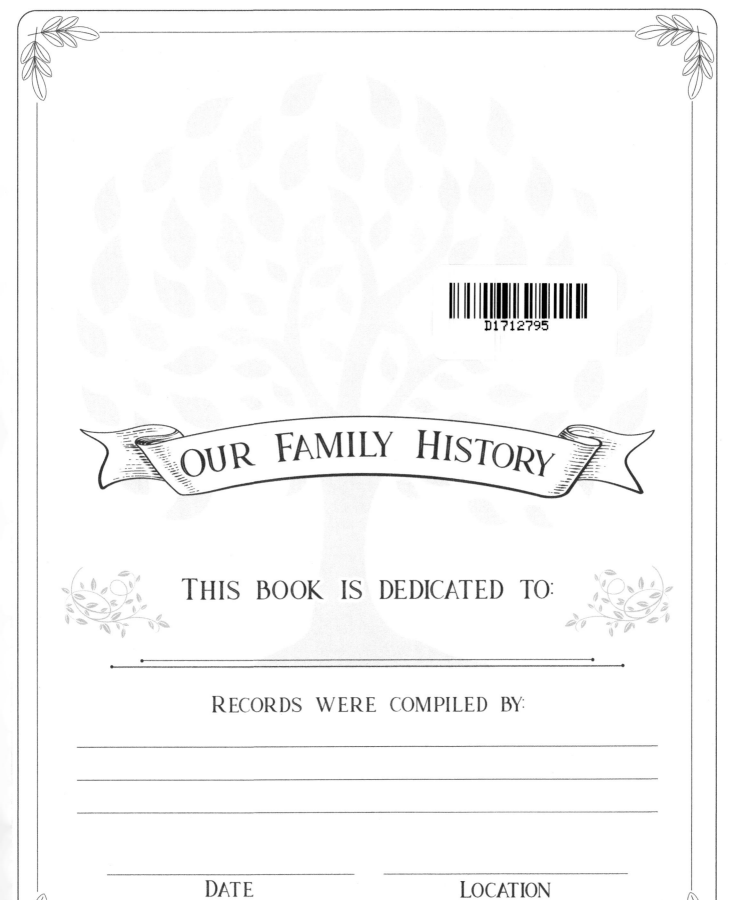

OUR FAMILY HISTORY

THIS BOOK IS DEDICATED TO:

_____

RECORDS WERE COMPILED BY:

_____

_____

_____

DATE   LOCATION

TABLE OF CONTENTS

FAMILY TREE
GENEALOGY CHART

HOW TO FILL IN THE CHART

START WITH A PRIMARY PERSON, FOR EXAMPLE YOURSELF, THEN IN THE CONNECTING BOXES ADD IN YOUR PARENTS NAMES. THEN IN THE TWO CONNECTING BOXES ADD IN THEIR PARENTS NAMES WHICH WOULD BE YOUR GRANDPARENTS. CONTINUE TO FILL IN THE NAMES UNTIL YOU REACHED THE END OF THE CHART. EACH CHART ALLOWS FOR SIX GENERATIONS OF FAMILY MEMBERS. TWO CHARTS ARE INCLUDED SO YOU CAN ALSO CHART YOUR SPOUSE'S GENEALOGY OR ANOTHER FAMILY MEMBER OF CHOICE.

AT THE BOTTOM OF EACH CHART YOU CAN FILL IN WHOM FILLED IN THE CHART AND THE DATE IT WAS COMPLETED. HAVE FUN LINKING TOGETHER THE FAMILY MEMBERS OF YOUR PAST!

FAMILY TREE

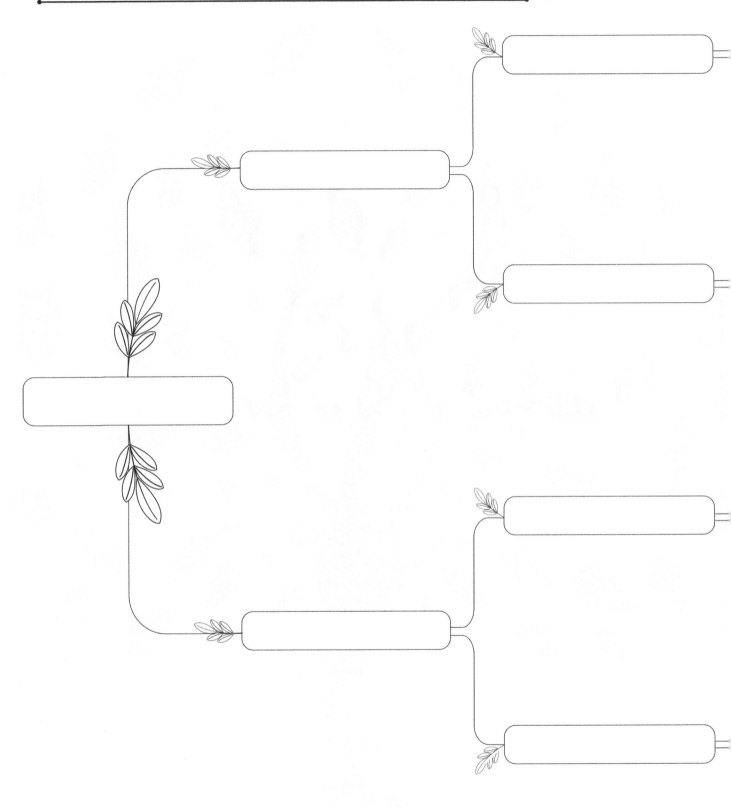

COMPLETED BY: _____

DATE: _____

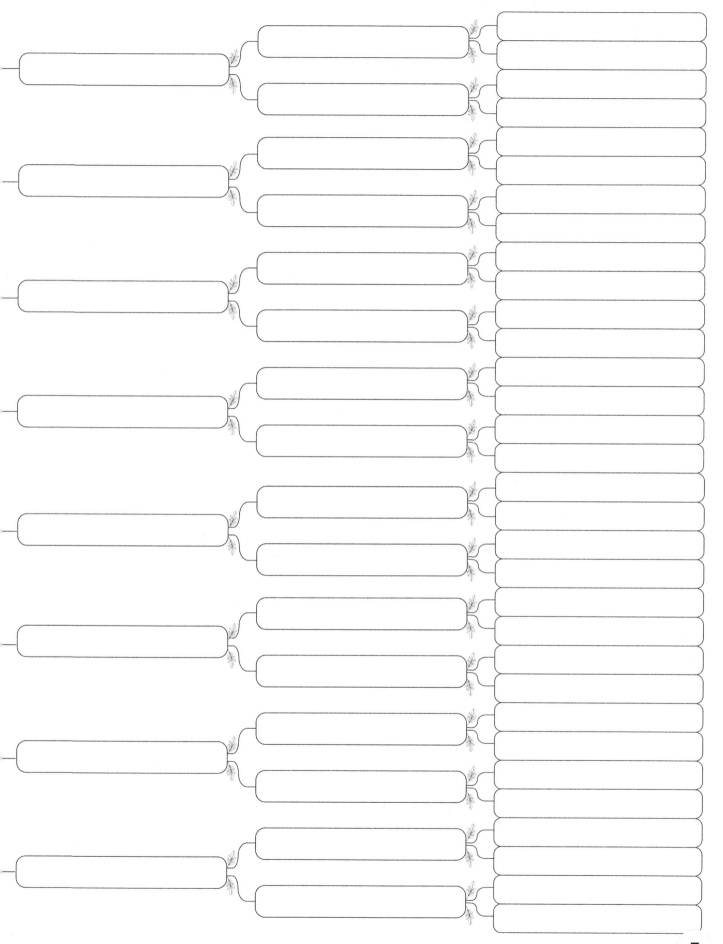

FAMILY TREE

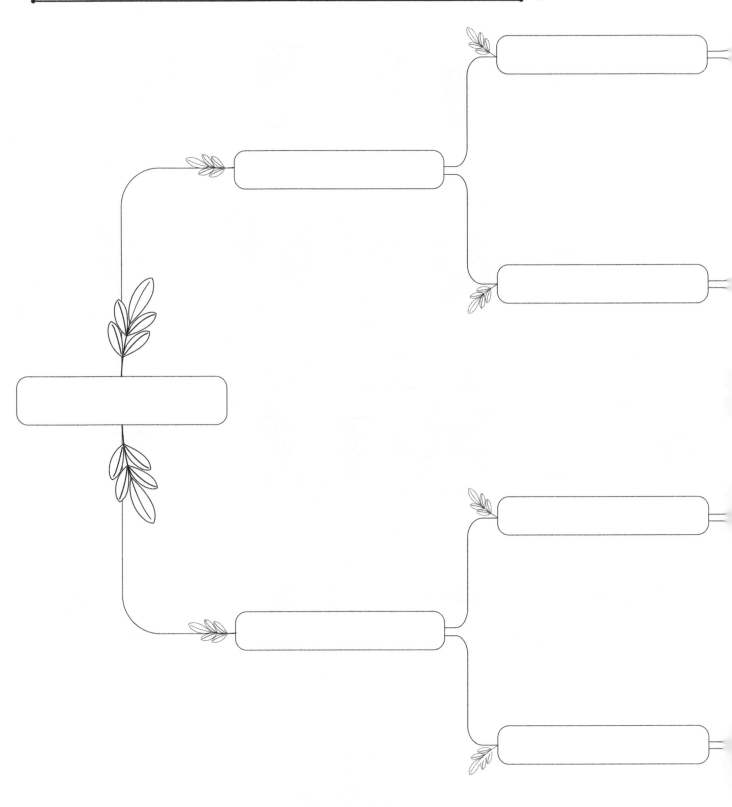

COMPLETED BY: _____ DATE: _____

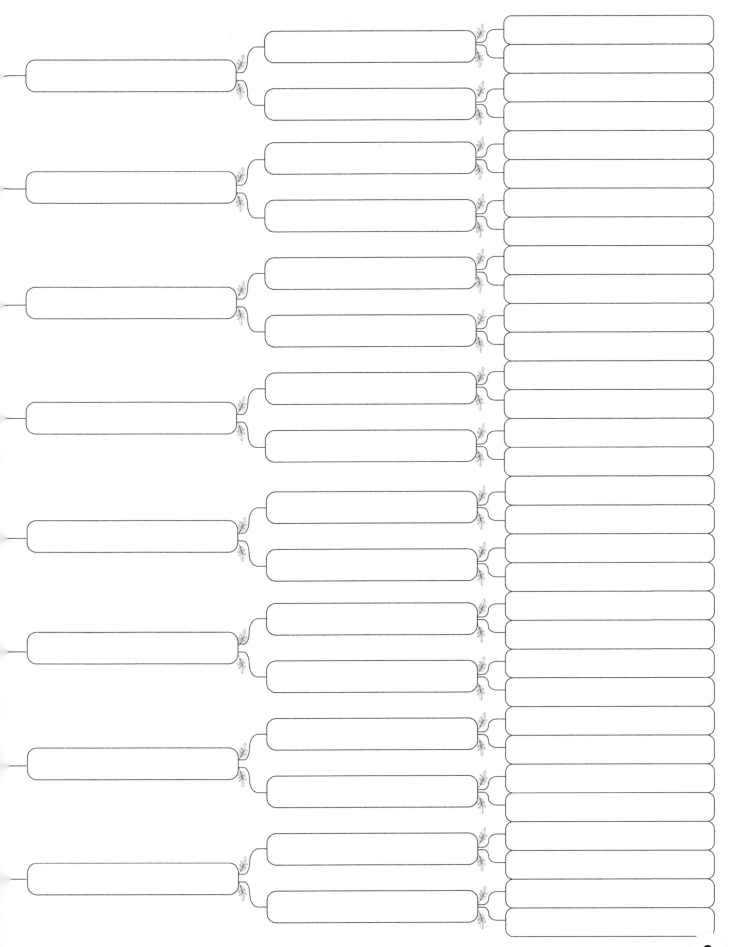

9

Family Traditions

NAME OF TRADITION _____ STARTED BY _____ PAGE _____

DETAILS: _____

_____

NAME OF TRADITION _____ STARTED BY _____ PAGE _____

DETAILS: _____

_____

NAME OF TRADITION _____ STARTED BY _____ PAGE _____

DETAILS: _____

_____

NAME OF TRADITION _____ STARTED BY _____ PAGE _____

DETAILS: _____

_____

NAME OF TRADITION _____ STARTED BY _____ PAGE _____

DETAILS: _____

_____

NAME OF TRADITION _____ STARTED BY _____ PAGE _____

DETAILS: _____

NAME OF TRADITION   STARTED BY   PAGE

DETAILS:

NAME OF TRADITION   STARTED BY   PAGE

DETAILS:

NAME OF TRADITION   STARTED BY   PAGE

DETAILS:

NAME OF TRADITION   STARTED BY   PAGE

DETAILS:

NAME OF TRADITION   STARTED BY   PAGE

DETAILS:

NAME OF TRADITION   STARTED BY   PAGE

DETAILS:

MILITARY SERVICE MEMBERS

NAME _____ PAGE _____ BRANCH OF SERVICE _____

GRADE \ RANK _____ YEARS OF SERVICE _____

DETAILS: AWARDS, DECORATIONS, TOURS _____

_____

_____

NAME _____ PAGE _____ BRANCH OF SERVICE _____

GRADE \ RANK _____ YEARS OF SERVICE _____

DETAILS: AWARDS, DECORATIONS, TOURS _____

_____

_____

NAME _____ PAGE _____ BRANCH OF SERVICE _____

GRADE \ RANK _____ YEARS OF SERVICE _____

DETAILS: AWARDS, DECORATIONS, TOURS _____

_____

_____

NAME _____ PAGE _____ BRANCH OF SERVICE _____

GRADE \ RANK _____ YEARS OF SERVICE _____

DETAILS: AWARDS, DECORATIONS, TOURS _____

_____

NAME

PAGE

BRANCH OF SERVICE

GRADE \ RANK

YEARS OF SERVICE

DETAILS: AWARDS, DECORATIONS. TOURS

NAME

PAGE

BRANCH OF SERVICE

GRADE \ RANK

YEARS OF SERVICE

DETAILS: AWARDS, DECORATIONS, TOURS

NAME

PAGE

BRANCH OF SERVICE

GRADE \ RANK

YEARS OF SERVICE

DETAILS: AWARDS, DECORATIONS, TOURS

NAME

PAGE

BRANCH OF SERVICE

GRADE \ RANK

YEARS OF SERVICE

DETAILS: AWARDS, DECORATIONS, TOURS

Beloved Pets

OWNER		PET NAME	TYPE OF PET	DATE
	PAGE			
	PAGE			
	PAGE			
	PAGE			
	PAGE			
	PAGE			
	PAGE			
	PAGE			
	PAGE			
	PAGE			
	PAGE			
	PAGE			
	PAGE			
	PAGE			

BELOVED PETS

OWNER	PET NAME	TYPE OF PET	DATE
_____ PAGE			
_____ PAGE			
_____ PAGE			
_____ PAGE			
_____ PAGE			
_____ PAGE			
_____ PAGE			
_____ PAGE			
_____ PAGE			
_____ PAGE			
_____ PAGE			
_____ PAGE			
_____ PAGE			

Places of Worship

PLACE OF WORSHIP NAME _____ YEARS ACTIVE _____

ADDRESS: _____

ATTENDED BY: _____

PLACE OF WORSHIP NAME _____ YEARS ACTIVE _____

ADDRESS: _____

ATTENDED BY: _____

PLACE OF WORSHIP NAME _____ YEARS ACTIVE _____

ADDRESS: _____

ATTENDED BY: _____

PLACE OF WORSHIP NAME _____ YEARS ACTIVE _____

ADDRESS: _____

ATTENDED BY: _____

PLACE OF WORSHIP NAME _____ YEARS ACTIVE _____

ADDRESS: _____

ATTENDED BY: _____

PLACE OF WORSHIP NAME _____ YEARS ACTIVE _____

ADDRESS: _____

ATTENDED BY: _____

PLACES OF WORSHIP

PLACE OF WORSHIP NAME

YEARS ACTIVE

ADDRESS:

ATTENDED BY:

PLACE OF WORSHIP NAME

YEARS ACTIVE

ADDRESS:

ATTENDED BY:

PLACE OF WORSHIP NAME

YEARS ACTIVE

ADDRESS:

ATTENDED BY:

PLACE OF WORSHIP NAME

YEARS ACTIVE

ADDRESS:

ATTENDED BY:

PLACE OF WORSHIP NAME

YEARS ACTIVE

ADDRESS:

ATTENDED BY:

PLACE OF WORSHIP NAME

YEARS ACTIVE

ADDRESS:

ATTENDED BY:

CLUB & ORGANIZATION MEMBERSHIPS

MEMBER OF

NAME OF MEMBER

PAGE

ADDRESS:

YEARS ACTIVE:

DETAILS:

MEMBER OF

NAME OF MEMBER

PAGE

ADDRESS:

YEARS ACTIVE:

DETAILS:

MEMBER OF

NAME OF MEMBER

PAGE

ADDRESS:

YEARS ACTIVE:

DETAILS:

MEMBER OF

NAME OF MEMBER

PAGE

ADDRESS:

YEARS ACTIVE:

DETAILS:

MEMBER OF

NAME OF MEMBER

PAGE

ADDRESS:

YEARS ACTIVE:

DETAILS:

MEMBER OF

NAME OF MEMBER

PAGE

ADDRESS:

YEARS ACTIVE:

DETAILS:

CLUB & ORGANIZATION MEMBERSHIPS

MEMBER OF

NAME OF MEMBER

PAGE

ADDRESS:

YEARS ACTIVE:

DETAILS:

MEMBER OF

NAME OF MEMBER

PAGE

ADDRESS:

YEARS ACTIVE:

DETAILS:

MEMBER OF

NAME OF MEMBER

PAGE

ADDRESS:

YEARS ACTIVE:

DETAILS:

MEMBER OF

NAME OF MEMBER

PAGE

ADDRESS:

YEARS ACTIVE:

DETAILS:

MEMBER OF

NAME OF MEMBER

PAGE

ADDRESS:

YEARS ACTIVE:

DETAILS:

MEMBER OF

NAME OF MEMBER

PAGE

ADDRESS:

YEARS ACTIVE:

DETAILS:

VEHICLES OWNED

MAKE & MODEL OF VEHICLE

NAME OF OWNER

PAGE

COLOR (S):

YEAR OF MAKE :

PURCHASE PRICE:

DETAILS:

MAKE & MODEL OF VEHICLE

NAME OF OWNER

PAGE

COLOR (S):

YEAR OF MAKE :

PURCHASE PRICE:

DETAILS:

MAKE & MODEL OF VEHICLE

NAME OF OWNER

PAGE

COLOR (S):

YEAR OF MAKE :

PURCHASE PRICE:

DETAILS:

MAKE & MODEL OF VEHICLE

NAME OF OWNER

PAGE

COLOR (S):

YEAR OF MAKE :

PURCHASE PRICE:

DETAILS:

MAKE & MODEL OF VEHICLE

NAME OF OWNER

PAGE

COLOR (S):

YEAR OF MAKE :

PURCHASE PRICE:

DETAILS:

MAKE & MODEL OF VEHICLE

NAME OF OWNER

PAGE

COLOR (S):

YEAR OF MAKE :

PURCHASE PRICE:

DETAILS:

MAKE & MODEL OF VEHICLE

NAME OF OWNER

PAGE

COLOR (S):

YEAR OF MAKE :

PURCHASE PRICE:

DETAILS:

MAKE & MODEL OF VEHICLE

NAME OF OWNER

PAGE

COLOR (S):

YEAR OF MAKE :

PURCHASE PRICE:

DETAILS:

MAKE & MODEL OF VEHICLE

NAME OF OWNER

PAGE

COLOR (S):

YEAR OF MAKE :

PURCHASE PRICE:

DETAILS:

MAKE & MODEL OF VEHICLE

NAME OF OWNER

PAGE

COLOR (S):

YEAR OF MAKE :

PURCHASE PRICE:

DETAILS:

MAKE & MODEL OF VEHICLE

NAME OF OWNER

PAGE

COLOR (S):

YEAR OF MAKE :

PURCHASE PRICE:

DETAILS:

MAKE & MODEL OF VEHICLE

NAME OF OWNER

PAGE

COLOR (S):

YEAR OF MAKE :

PURCHASE PRICE:

DETAILS:

KNOWN FAMILY ILLNESSES

NAME _____ PAGE _____ ILLNESS /OPERATION _____

DETAILS: _____

_____

NAME _____ PAGE _____ ILLNESS /OPERATION _____

DETAILS: _____

_____

NAME _____ PAGE _____ ILLNESS /OPERATION _____

DETAILS: _____

_____

NAME _____ PAGE _____ ILLNESS /OPERATION _____

DETAILS: _____

_____

NAME _____ PAGE _____ ILLNESS /OPERATION _____

DETAILS: _____

_____

NAME _____ PAGE _____ ILLNESS /OPERATION _____

DETAILS: _____

NAME _____ PAGE _____ ILLNESS /OPERATION _____

DETAILS: _____

_____

NAME _____ PAGE _____ ILLNESS /OPERATION _____

DETAILS: _____

_____

NAME _____ PAGE _____ ILLNESS /OPERATION _____

DETAILS: _____

_____

NAME _____ PAGE _____ ILLNESS /OPERATION _____

DETAILS: _____

_____

NAME _____ PAGE _____ ILLNESS /OPERATION _____

DETAILS: _____

_____

NAME _____ PAGE _____ ILLNESS /OPERATION _____

DETAILS: _____

NOTABLE FAMILY EVENTS

OCCASION _____   DATE _____   LOCATION _____

DETAILS: _____

_____

_____

OCCASION _____   DATE _____   LOCATION _____

DETAILS: _____

_____

_____

OCCASION _____   DATE _____   LOCATION _____

DETAILS: _____

_____

_____

OCCASION _____   DATE _____   LOCATION _____

DETAILS: _____

_____

_____

OCCASION _____   DATE _____   LOCATION _____

DETAILS: _____

_____

_____

OCCASION _____   DATE _____   LOCATION _____

DETAILS: _____

OCCASION _____ DATE _____ LOCATION _____

DETAILS: _____

OCCASION _____ DATE _____ LOCATION _____

DETAILS: _____

OCCASION _____ DATE _____ LOCATION _____

DETAILS: _____

OCCASION _____ DATE _____ LOCATION _____

DETAILS: _____

OCCASION _____ DATE _____ LOCATION _____

DETAILS: _____

OCCASION _____ DATE _____ LOCATION _____

DETAILS: _____

FAMILY

PHOTOS

FAMILY

PHOTOS

FAMILY

PHOTOS

Treasured Family Recipes

RECIPE:

RECIPE FROM: _____ PAGE _____

PREP TIME _____   COOK TIME _____   SERVINGS _____

INGREDIENTS

_____
_____
_____
_____
_____
_____

DIRECTIONS

_____
_____
_____
_____
_____
_____
_____
_____
_____
_____

NOTES: _____
_____
_____

RECIPE:

RECIPE FROM: _____ PAGE _____

PREP TIME _____ COOK TIME _____ SERVINGS _____

— INGREDIENTS —

_____   _____
_____   _____
_____   _____
_____   _____
_____   _____
_____   _____

— DIRECTIONS —

_____
_____
_____
_____
_____
_____
_____
_____
_____
_____
_____
_____

NOTES:
_____
_____
_____

RECIPE:

RECIPE FROM: _____ PAGE _____

PREP TIME   COOK TIME   SERVINGS

INGREDIENTS

_____ _____
_____ _____
_____ _____
_____ _____
_____ _____
_____ _____

DIRECTIONS

_____
_____
_____
_____
_____
_____
_____
_____
_____
_____
_____

NOTES:
_____
_____

RECIPE:

RECIPE FROM: _____ PAGE _____

PREP TIME   COOK TIME   SERVINGS

INGREDIENTS

_____   _____
_____   _____
_____   _____
_____   _____
_____   _____
_____   _____
_____   _____

DIRECTIONS

_____
_____
_____
_____
_____
_____
_____
_____
_____
_____
_____
_____

NOTES:
_____
_____
_____

RECIPE:

RECIPE FROM: _____ PAGE _____

PREP TIME _____ COOK TIME _____ SERVINGS _____

INGREDIENTS

_____   _____
_____   _____
_____   _____
_____   _____
_____   _____
_____   _____
_____   _____

DIRECTIONS

_____
_____
_____
_____
_____
_____
_____
_____
_____
_____
_____

NOTES:

_____
_____

RECIPE:

RECIPE FROM: _____ PAGE _____

PREP TIME _____ COOK TIME _____ SERVINGS _____

INGREDIENTS

_____   _____
_____   _____
_____   _____
_____   _____
_____   _____
_____   _____
_____   _____

DIRECTIONS

_____
_____
_____
_____
_____
_____
_____
_____
_____
_____
_____
_____

NOTES:
_____
_____
_____

RECIPE:

RECIPE FROM: _____ PAGE _____

PREP TIME _____ COOK TIME _____ SERVINGS _____

INGREDIENTS

_____   _____
_____   _____
_____   _____
_____   _____
_____   _____
_____   _____

DIRECTIONS

_____
_____
_____
_____
_____
_____
_____
_____
_____
_____

NOTES:
_____
_____

RECIPE:

RECIPE FROM: _____ PAGE _____

 _____ PREP TIME _____ COOK TIME _____ SERVINGS

INGREDIENTS

_____ _____
_____ _____
_____ _____
_____ _____
_____ _____
_____ _____

DIRECTIONS

_____
_____
_____
_____
_____
_____
_____
_____
_____
_____

NOTES:
_____
_____
_____

RECIPE:

RECIPE FROM: _____ PAGE _____

PREP TIME _____ COOK TIME _____ SERVINGS _____

INGREDIENTS

_____   _____
_____   _____
_____   _____
_____   _____
_____   _____
_____   _____
_____   _____

DIRECTIONS

_____
_____
_____
_____
_____
_____
_____
_____
_____
_____
_____
_____

NOTES:
_____
_____
_____

RECIPE:

RECIPE FROM: _____ PAGE _____

PREP TIME _____ COOK TIME _____ SERVINGS _____

INGREDIENTS

_____
_____
_____
_____
_____
_____
_____

_____
_____
_____
_____
_____
_____
_____

DIRECTIONS

_____
_____
_____
_____
_____
_____
_____
_____
_____
_____
_____
_____

NOTES:
_____
_____
_____

Record of
Family
Members

THIS SECTION ALLOWS YOU TO KEEP A RECORD OF UP TO 100 FAMILY MEMBERS.

ONCE EACH PAGE IS COMPLETED OR AT MINIMUM CONTAINS THE NAME OF THE FAMILY MEMBER, YOU CAN THEN REFERENCE BACK TO THE PAGE NUMBER YOUR FAMILY MEMBER IS MENTIONED. FOR EXAMPLE ON THE VEHICLES RECORD SECTION, ON THE OWNER LINE INFO, YOU CAN INCLUDE THE OWNER'S PAGE NUMBER BACK TO THEIR RECORD PAGE.

AT BOTTOM OF EVERY FAMILY MEMBER'S RECORD PAGE YOU CAN MARK DOWN THE PAGE NUMBER FOR EVERY TIME THEY WERE MENTIONED. ADDITIONALLY YOU CAN LIST THEIR RECORD PAGE NUMBER ON THE INDEX OF FAMILY MEMBERS MAKING IT EASIER TO FIND FAMILY MEMBERS BY NAME.

A LINK BETWEEN THEIR ADDED INFORMATION IS CREATED. WITH EVERY REFERENCE BACK TO THEIR RECORD'S PAGE NUMBER, MAKING THEIR STORY MORE FULL!

_____ FATHER'S NAME | PAGE _____

_____ MOTHER'S NAME | PAGE _____

_____

NAME GIVEN AT BIRTH

_____
DATE OF BIRTH

_____
DATE OF DEATH

_____
PLACE OF BIRTH

_____
PLACE OF DEATH

_____
NAME OF SPOUSE | PAGE_____

_____
MARITAL STATUS & DATE OF MARRIAGE

_____
PLACE OF MARRIAGE

CHILDREN

_____
NAME | PAGE _____

_____
NAME | PAGE _____

_____
NAME | PAGE _____

_____
NAME | PAGE _____

_____
NAME | PAGE _____

_____
NAME | PAGE _____

_____
NAME | PAGE _____

_____
NAME | PAGE _____

_____
NAME | PAGE _____

_____
NAME | PAGE _____

NOTABLE CHARACTERISTICS & LIFE EVENTS:

_____

_____

_____

_____

ADDITIONAL SPOUSE | PAGE_____ || ADDITIONAL CHILDREN | PAGE_____

CHARTS INCLUDED IN | PAGE _____ || APPEARS IN PHOTOS | PAGE _____ || MENTIONED IN PAGES _____

FATHER'S NAME | PAGE _____

MOTHER'S NAME | PAGE _____

NAME GIVEN AT BIRTH

_____
DATE OF BIRTH

_____
PLACE OF BIRTH

_____
DATE OF DEATH

_____
PLACE OF DEATH

_____
NAME OF SPOUSE | PAGE_____

_____
MARITAL STATUS & DATE OF MARRIAGE

_____
PLACE OF MARRIAGE

CHILDREN

_____
NAME | PAGE _____

_____
NAME | PAGE _____

_____
NAME | PAGE _____

_____
NAME | PAGE _____

_____
NAME | PAGE _____

_____
NAME | PAGE _____

_____
NAME | PAGE _____

_____
NAME | PAGE _____

_____
NAME | PAGE _____

_____
NAME | PAGE _____

NOTABLE CHARACTERISTICS & LIFE EVENTS:

_____

_____

_____

_____

_____

FATHER'S NAME | PAGE _____

_____

MOTHER'S NAME | PAGE _____

_____

NAME GIVEN AT BIRTH

_____
DATE OF BIRTH

_____
DATE OF DEATH

_____
PLACE OF BIRTH

_____
PLACE OF DEATH

_____
NAME OF SPOUSE | PAGE_____

_____
MARITAL STATUS & DATE OF MARRIAGE

_____
PLACE OF MARRIAGE

CHILDREN

_____
NAME | PAGE _____

_____
NAME | PAGE _____

_____
NAME | PAGE _____

_____
NAME | PAGE _____

_____
NAME | PAGE _____

_____
NAME | PAGE _____

_____
NAME | PAGE _____

_____
NAME | PAGE _____

_____
NAME | PAGE _____

_____
NAME | PAGE _____

NOTABLE CHARACTERISTICS & LIFE EVENTS: _____

_____

_____

_____

ADDITIONAL SPOUSE | PAGE_____ || ADDITIONAL CHILDREN | PAGE_____

CHARTS INCLUDED IN | PAGE _____ || APPEARS IN PHOTOS | PAGE _____ || MENTIONED IN PAGES _____

_____
FATHER'S NAME | PAGE _____

_____
MOTHER'S NAME | PAGE _____

_____

NAME GIVEN AT BIRTH

_____
DATE OF BIRTH

_____
DATE OF DEATH

_____
PLACE OF BIRTH

_____
PLACE OF DEATH

_____
NAME OF SPOUSE | PAGE_____

_____
MARITAL STATUS & DATE OF MARRIAGE

_____
PLACE OF MARRIAGE

CHILDREN

_____
NAME | PAGE _____

_____
NAME | PAGE _____

_____
NAME | PAGE _____

_____
NAME | PAGE _____

_____
NAME | PAGE _____

_____
NAME | PAGE _____

_____
NAME | PAGE _____

_____
NAME | PAGE _____

_____
NAME | PAGE _____

_____
NAME | PAGE _____

NOTABLE CHARACTERISTICS & LIFE EVENTS:

_____

_____

_____

_____

ADDITIONAL SPOUSE | PAGE_____ || ADDITIONAL CHILDREN | PAGE_____

_____
FATHER'S NAME | PAGE _____

_____
MOTHER'S NAME | PAGE _____

_____

NAME GIVEN AT BIRTH

_____
DATE OF BIRTH

_____
DATE OF DEATH

_____
PLACE OF BIRTH

_____
PLACE OF DEATH

_____
NAME OF SPOUSE | PAGE_____

_____
MARITAL STATUS & DATE OF MARRIAGE

_____
PLACE OF MARRIAGE

CHILDREN

_____
NAME | PAGE _____

_____
NAME | PAGE _____

_____
NAME | PAGE _____

_____
NAME | PAGE _____

_____
NAME | PAGE _____

_____
NAME | PAGE _____

_____
NAME | PAGE _____

_____
NAME | PAGE _____

_____
NAME | PAGE _____

_____
NAME | PAGE _____

NOTABLE CHARACTERISTICS & LIFE EVENTS:
_____
_____
_____
_____

ADDITIONAL SPOUSE | PAGE_____ || ADDITIONAL CHILDREN | PAGE_____

CHARTS INCLUDED IN | PAGE _____ || APPEARS IN PHOTOS | PAGE _____ || MENTIONED IN PAGES _____

_____ | FATHER'S NAME | PAGE _____

_____ | MOTHER'S NAME | PAGE _____

NAME GIVEN AT BIRTH

_____
DATE OF BIRTH

_____
PLACE OF BIRTH

_____
DATE OF DEATH

_____
PLACE OF DEATH

_____
NAME OF SPOUSE | PAGE _____

_____
MARITAL STATUS & DATE OF MARRIAGE

_____
PLACE OF MARRIAGE

CHILDREN

_____
NAME | PAGE _____

_____
NAME | PAGE _____

_____
NAME | PAGE _____

_____
NAME | PAGE _____

_____
NAME | PAGE _____

_____
NAME | PAGE _____

_____
NAME | PAGE _____

_____
NAME | PAGE _____

_____
NAME | PAGE _____

_____
NAME | PAGE _____

NOTABLE CHARACTERISTICS & LIFE EVENTS: _____

_____

_____

_____

ADDITIONAL SPOUSE | PAGE _____ || ADDITIONAL CHILDREN | PAGE _____

FATHER'S NAME | PAGE ____

MOTHER'S NAME | PAGE ____

NAME GIVEN AT BIRTH

_____
DATE OF BIRTH

_____
DATE OF DEATH

_____
PLACE OF BIRTH

_____
PLACE OF DEATH

_____
NAME OF SPOUSE | PAGE_____

_____
MARITAL STATUS & DATE OF MARRIAGE

_____
PLACE OF MARRIAGE

CHILDREN

NAME | PAGE ____	NAME | PAGE ____
NAME | PAGE ____	NAME | PAGE ____
NAME | PAGE ____	NAME | PAGE ____
NAME | PAGE ____	NAME | PAGE ____
NAME | PAGE ____	NAME | PAGE ____

NOTABLE CHARACTERISTICS & LIFE EVENTS:

_____

_____

_____

ADDITIONAL SPOUSE | PAGE_____ || ADDITIONAL CHILDREN | PAGE_____

CHARTS INCLUDED IN | PAGE _____ || APPEARS IN PHOTOS | PAGE _____ || MENTIONED IN PAGES _____

FATHER'S NAME | PAGE _____

MOTHER'S NAME | PAGE _____

NAME GIVEN AT BIRTH

DATE OF BIRTH

DATE OF DEATH

PLACE OF BIRTH

PLACE OF DEATH

NAME OF SPOUSE | PAGE _____

MARITAL STATUS & DATE OF MARRIAGE

PLACE OF MARRIAGE

CHILDREN

NAME | PAGE _____

NAME | PAGE _____

NAME | PAGE _____

NAME | PAGE _____

NAME | PAGE _____

NAME | PAGE _____

NAME | PAGE _____

NAME | PAGE _____

NAME | PAGE _____

NAME | PAGE _____

NOTABLE CHARACTERISTICS & LIFE EVENTS:

ADDITIONAL SPOUSE | PAGE_____ || ADDITIONAL CHILDREN | PAGE_____

_____

FATHER'S NAME | PAGE _____

_____

MOTHER'S NAME | PAGE _____

NAME GIVEN AT BIRTH

_____

DATE OF BIRTH

_____

DATE OF DEATH

_____

PLACE OF BIRTH

_____

PLACE OF DEATH

_____

NAME OF SPOUSE | PAGE_____

_____

MARITAL STATUS & DATE OF MARRIAGE

_____

PLACE OF MARRIAGE

CHILDREN

_____

NAME | PAGE _____

_____

NAME | PAGE _____

_____

NAME | PAGE _____

_____

NAME | PAGE _____

_____

NAME | PAGE _____

_____

NAME | PAGE _____

_____

NAME | PAGE _____

_____

NAME | PAGE _____

_____

NAME | PAGE _____

_____

NAME | PAGE _____

NOTABLE CHARACTERISTICS & LIFE EVENTS:

_____

_____

_____

_____

_____   _____

FATHER'S NAME | PAGE _____   MOTHER'S NAME | PAGE _____

_____

NAME GIVEN AT BIRTH

_____   _____

DATE OF BIRTH   DATE OF DEATH

_____   _____

PLACE OF BIRTH   PLACE OF DEATH

_____

NAME OF SPOUSE | PAGE_____

_____   _____

MARITAL STATUS & DATE OF MARRIAGE   PLACE OF MARRIAGE

CHILDREN

_____   _____

NAME | PAGE _____   NAME | PAGE _____

_____   _____

NAME | PAGE _____   NAME | PAGE _____

_____   _____

NAME | PAGE _____   NAME | PAGE _____

_____   _____

NAME | PAGE _____   NAME | PAGE _____

_____   _____

NAME | PAGE _____   NAME | PAGE _____

NOTABLE CHARACTERISTICS & LIFE EVENTS: _____

_____

_____

_____

_____

ADDITIONAL SPOUSE | PAGE_____ || ADDITIONAL CHILDREN | PAGE_____

CHARTS INCLUDED IN | PAGE _____ || APPEARS IN PHOTOS | PAGE _____ || MENTIONED IN PAGES _____

_____
FATHER'S NAME | PAGE _____

_____
MOTHER'S NAME | PAGE _____

_____

NAME GIVEN AT BIRTH

_____
DATE OF BIRTH

_____
DATE OF DEATH

_____
PLACE OF BIRTH

_____
PLACE OF DEATH

_____
NAME OF SPOUSE | PAGE_____

_____
MARITAL STATUS & DATE OF MARRIAGE

_____
PLACE OF MARRIAGE

CHILDREN

_____
NAME | PAGE _____

_____
NAME | PAGE _____

_____
NAME | PAGE _____

_____
NAME | PAGE _____

_____
NAME | PAGE _____

_____
NAME | PAGE _____

_____
NAME | PAGE _____

_____
NAME | PAGE _____

_____
NAME | PAGE _____

_____
NAME | PAGE _____

NOTABLE CHARACTERISTICS & LIFE EVENTS:

_____
_____
_____
_____

ADDITIONAL SPOUSE | PAGE_____ || ADDITIONAL CHILDREN | PAGE_____

CHARTS INCLUDED IN | PAGE _____ || APPEARS IN PHOTOS | PAGE _____ || MENTIONED IN PAGES _____

_____

FATHER'S NAME | PAGE _____

_____

MOTHER'S NAME | PAGE _____

_____

NAME GIVEN AT BIRTH

_____
DATE OF BIRTH

_____
DATE OF DEATH

_____
PLACE OF BIRTH

_____
PLACE OF DEATH

_____
NAME OF SPOUSE | PAGE_____

_____
MARITAL STATUS & DATE OF MARRIAGE

_____
PLACE OF MARRIAGE

CHILDREN

_____
NAME | PAGE _____

_____
NAME | PAGE _____

_____
NAME | PAGE _____

_____
NAME | PAGE _____

_____
NAME | PAGE _____

_____
NAME | PAGE _____

_____
NAME | PAGE _____

_____
NAME | PAGE _____

_____
NAME | PAGE _____

_____
NAME | PAGE _____

NOTABLE CHARACTERISTICS & LIFE EVENTS: _____

_____

_____

_____

ADDITIONAL SPOUSE | PAGE_____ || ADDITIONAL CHILDREN | PAGE_____

CHARTS INCLUDED IN | PAGE _____ || APPEARS IN PHOTOS | PAGE _____ || MENTIONED IN PAGES _____

_____

FATHER'S NAME | PAGE _____

_____

MOTHER'S NAME | PAGE _____

_____

NAME GIVEN AT BIRTH

_____

DATE OF BIRTH

_____

DATE OF DEATH

_____

PLACE OF BIRTH

_____

PLACE OF DEATH

_____

NAME OF SPOUSE | PAGE_____

_____

MARITAL STATUS & DATE OF MARRIAGE

_____

PLACE OF MARRIAGE

CHILDREN

_____

NAME | PAGE _____

_____

NAME | PAGE _____

_____

NAME | PAGE _____

_____

NAME | PAGE _____

_____

NAME | PAGE _____

_____

NAME | PAGE _____

_____

NAME | PAGE _____

_____

NAME | PAGE _____

_____

NAME | PAGE _____

_____

NAME | PAGE _____

NOTABLE CHARACTERISTICS & LIFE EVENTS:

_____
_____
_____
_____

ADDITIONAL SPOUSE | PAGE_____ || ADDITIONAL CHILDREN | PAGE_____

CHARTS INCLUDED IN | PAGE _____ || APPEARS IN PHOTOS | PAGE _____ || MENTIONED IN PAGES _____

FATHER'S NAME | PAGE _____

MOTHER'S NAME | PAGE _____

NAME GIVEN AT BIRTH

_____
DATE OF BIRTH

_____
DATE OF DEATH

_____
PLACE OF BIRTH

_____
PLACE OF DEATH

_____
NAME OF SPOUSE | PAGE _____

_____
MARITAL STATUS & DATE OF MARRIAGE

_____
PLACE OF MARRIAGE

CHILDREN

_____
NAME | PAGE _____

_____
NAME | PAGE _____

_____
NAME | PAGE _____

_____
NAME | PAGE _____

_____
NAME | PAGE _____

_____
NAME | PAGE _____

_____
NAME | PAGE _____

_____
NAME | PAGE _____

_____
NAME | PAGE _____

_____
NAME | PAGE _____

NOTABLE CHARACTERISTICS & LIFE EVENTS:

_____

_____

_____

_____

ADDITIONAL SPOUSE | PAGE _____ || ADDITIONAL CHILDREN | PAGE _____

_____

FATHER'S NAME | PAGE _____

_____

MOTHER'S NAME | PAGE _____

_____

NAME GIVEN AT BIRTH

_____
DATE OF BIRTH

_____
DATE OF DEATH

_____
PLACE OF BIRTH

_____
PLACE OF DEATH

_____
NAME OF SPOUSE | PAGE_____

_____
MARITAL STATUS & DATE OF MARRIAGE

_____
PLACE OF MARRIAGE

CHILDREN

_____
NAME | PAGE _____

_____
NAME | PAGE _____

_____
NAME | PAGE _____

_____
NAME | PAGE _____

_____
NAME | PAGE _____

_____
NAME | PAGE _____

_____
NAME | PAGE _____

_____
NAME | PAGE _____

_____
NAME | PAGE _____

_____
NAME | PAGE _____

NOTABLE CHARACTERISTICS & LIFE EVENTS:

_____

_____

_____

_____

ADDITIONAL SPOUSE | PAGE_____ || ADDITIONAL CHILDREN | PAGE_____

CHARTS INCLUDED IN | PAGE _____ || APPEARS IN PHOTOS | PAGE _____ || MENTIONED IN PAGES _____

_____

FATHER'S NAME | PAGE _____

_____

MOTHER'S NAME | PAGE _____

_____

NAME GIVEN AT BIRTH

_____
DATE OF BIRTH

_____
DATE OF DEATH

_____
PLACE OF BIRTH

_____
PLACE OF DEATH

_____
NAME OF SPOUSE | PAGE_____

_____
MARITAL STATUS & DATE OF MARRIAGE

_____
PLACE OF MARRIAGE

CHILDREN

_____
NAME | PAGE _____

_____
NAME | PAGE _____

_____
NAME | PAGE _____

_____
NAME | PAGE _____

_____
NAME | PAGE _____

_____
NAME | PAGE _____

_____
NAME | PAGE _____

_____
NAME | PAGE _____

_____
NAME | PAGE _____

_____
NAME | PAGE _____

NOTABLE CHARACTERISTICS & LIFE EVENTS:

_____

_____

_____

_____

ADDITIONAL SPOUSE | PAGE_____ || ADDITIONAL CHILDREN | PAGE_____

CHARTS INCLUDED IN | PAGE _____ || APPEARS IN PHOTOS | PAGE _____ || MENTIONED IN PAGES _____

_____
FATHER'S NAME | PAGE _____

_____
MOTHER'S NAME | PAGE _____

_____

NAME GIVEN AT BIRTH

_____
DATE OF BIRTH

_____
DATE OF DEATH

_____
PLACE OF BIRTH

_____
PLACE OF DEATH

_____
NAME OF SPOUSE | PAGE_____

_____
MARITAL STATUS & DATE OF MARRIAGE

_____
PLACE OF MARRIAGE

CHILDREN

_____
NAME | PAGE _____

_____
NAME | PAGE _____

_____
NAME | PAGE _____

_____
NAME | PAGE _____

_____
NAME | PAGE _____

_____
NAME | PAGE _____

_____
NAME | PAGE _____

_____
NAME | PAGE _____

_____
NAME | PAGE _____

_____
NAME | PAGE _____

NOTABLE CHARACTERISTICS & LIFE EVENTS:

_____

_____

_____

_____

ADDITIONAL SPOUSE | PAGE_____ || ADDITIONAL CHILDREN | PAGE_____

_____

FATHER'S NAME | PAGE _____   MOTHER'S NAME | PAGE _____

_____

NAME GIVEN AT BIRTH

_____   _____
DATE OF BIRTH   DATE OF DEATH

_____   _____
PLACE OF BIRTH   PLACE OF DEATH

_____
NAME OF SPOUSE | PAGE _____

_____   _____
MARITAL STATUS & DATE OF MARRIAGE   PLACE OF MARRIAGE

CHILDREN

_____   _____
NAME | PAGE _____   NAME | PAGE _____

_____   _____
NAME | PAGE _____   NAME | PAGE _____

_____   _____
NAME | PAGE _____   NAME | PAGE _____

_____   _____
NAME | PAGE _____   NAME | PAGE _____

_____   _____
NAME | PAGE _____   NAME | PAGE _____

NOTABLE CHARACTERISTICS & LIFE EVENTS: _____

_____

_____

_____

ADDITIONAL SPOUSE | PAGE _____ || ADDITIONAL CHILDREN | PAGE _____

CHARTS INCLUDED IN | PAGE _____ || APPEARS IN PHOTOS | PAGE _____ || MENTIONED IN PAGES _____

_____

FATHER'S NAME | PAGE _____

_____

MOTHER'S NAME | PAGE _____

_____

NAME GIVEN AT BIRTH

_____
DATE OF BIRTH

_____
DATE OF DEATH

_____
PLACE OF BIRTH

_____
PLACE OF DEATH

_____
NAME OF SPOUSE | PAGE_____

_____
MARITAL STATUS & DATE OF MARRIAGE

_____
PLACE OF MARRIAGE

CHILDREN

_____
NAME | PAGE _____

_____
NAME | PAGE _____

_____
NAME | PAGE _____

_____
NAME | PAGE _____

_____
NAME | PAGE _____

_____
NAME | PAGE _____

_____
NAME | PAGE _____

_____
NAME | PAGE _____

_____
NAME | PAGE _____

_____
NAME | PAGE _____

NOTABLE CHARACTERISTICS & LIFE EVENTS: _____

_____

_____

_____

ADDITIONAL SPOUSE | PAGE_____ || ADDITIONAL CHILDREN | PAGE_____

CHARTS INCLUDED IN | PAGE _____ || APPEARS IN PHOTOS | PAGE _____ || MENTIONED IN PAGES _____

FATHER'S NAME | PAGE _____

MOTHER'S NAME | PAGE _____

NAME GIVEN AT BIRTH

_____
DATE OF BIRTH

_____
PLACE OF BIRTH

_____
DATE OF DEATH

_____
PLACE OF DEATH

_____
NAME OF SPOUSE | PAGE_____

_____
MARITAL STATUS & DATE OF MARRIAGE

_____
PLACE OF MARRIAGE

CHILDREN

_____
NAME | PAGE _____

_____
NAME | PAGE _____

_____
NAME | PAGE _____

_____
NAME | PAGE _____

_____
NAME | PAGE _____

_____
NAME | PAGE _____

_____
NAME | PAGE _____

_____
NAME | PAGE _____

_____
NAME | PAGE _____

_____
NAME | PAGE _____

NOTABLE CHARACTERISTICS & LIFE EVENTS: _____

_____

_____

_____

ADDITIONAL SPOUSE | PAGE_____ || ADDITIONAL CHILDREN | PAGE_____

CHARTS INCLUDED IN | PAGE _____ || APPEARS IN PHOTOS | PAGE _____ || MENTIONED IN PAGES _____

_____
FATHER'S NAME | PAGE _____

_____
MOTHER'S NAME | PAGE _____

NAME GIVEN AT BIRTH

_____
DATE OF BIRTH

_____
PLACE OF BIRTH

_____
DATE OF DEATH

_____
PLACE OF DEATH

_____
NAME OF SPOUSE | PAGE _____

_____
MARITAL STATUS & DATE OF MARRIAGE

_____
PLACE OF MARRIAGE

CHILDREN

_____
NAME | PAGE _____

_____
NAME | PAGE _____

_____
NAME | PAGE _____

_____
NAME | PAGE _____

_____
NAME | PAGE _____

_____
NAME | PAGE _____

_____
NAME | PAGE _____

_____
NAME | PAGE _____

_____
NAME | PAGE _____

_____
NAME | PAGE _____

NOTABLE CHARACTERISTICS & LIFE EVENTS:
_____
_____
_____
_____

ADDITIONAL SPOUSE | PAGE_____ || ADDITIONAL CHILDREN | PAGE_____

CHARTS INCLUDED IN | PAGE _____ || APPEARS IN PHOTOS | PAGE _____ || MENTIONED IN PAGES _____

_____ | _____

FATHER'S NAME | PAGE _____ | MOTHER'S NAME | PAGE _____

_____

NAME GIVEN AT BIRTH

_____ | _____

DATE OF BIRTH | DATE OF DEATH

_____ | _____

PLACE OF BIRTH | PLACE OF DEATH

_____

NAME OF SPOUSE | PAGE_____

_____ | _____

MARITAL STATUS & DATE OF MARRIAGE | PLACE OF MARRIAGE

CHILDREN

NAME | PAGE _____ | NAME | PAGE _____

NAME | PAGE _____ | NAME | PAGE _____

NAME | PAGE _____ | NAME | PAGE _____

NAME | PAGE _____ | NAME | PAGE _____

NAME | PAGE _____ | NAME | PAGE _____

NOTABLE CHARACTERISTICS & LIFE EVENTS:

_____

_____

_____

_____

ADDITIONAL SPOUSE | PAGE_____ || ADDITIONAL CHILDREN | PAGE_____

FATHER'S NAME | PAGE _____

MOTHER'S NAME | PAGE _____

NAME GIVEN AT BIRTH

_____

DATE OF BIRTH

_____

PLACE OF BIRTH

_____

DATE OF DEATH

_____

PLACE OF DEATH

_____

NAME OF SPOUSE | PAGE_____

_____
MARITAL STATUS & DATE OF MARRIAGE

_____
PLACE OF MARRIAGE

CHILDREN

NAME | PAGE _____

NAME | PAGE _____

NAME | PAGE _____

NAME | PAGE _____

NAME | PAGE _____

NAME | PAGE _____

NAME | PAGE _____

NAME | PAGE _____

NAME | PAGE _____

NAME | PAGE _____

NOTABLE CHARACTERISTICS & LIFE EVENTS: _____

_____

_____

_____

ADDITIONAL SPOUSE | PAGE_____ || ADDITIONAL CHILDREN | PAGE_____

CHARTS INCLUDED IN | PAGE _____ || APPEARS IN PHOTOS | PAGE _____ || MENTIONED IN PAGES _____

_____
FATHER'S NAME | PAGE _____

_____
MOTHER'S NAME | PAGE _____

_____

NAME GIVEN AT BIRTH

_____
DATE OF BIRTH

_____
DATE OF DEATH

_____
PLACE OF BIRTH

_____
PLACE OF DEATH

_____
NAME OF SPOUSE | PAGE_____

_____
MARITAL STATUS & DATE OF MARRIAGE

_____
PLACE OF MARRIAGE

CHILDREN

_____
NAME | PAGE _____

_____
NAME | PAGE _____

_____
NAME | PAGE _____

_____
NAME | PAGE _____

_____
NAME | PAGE _____

_____
NAME | PAGE _____

_____
NAME | PAGE _____

_____
NAME | PAGE _____

_____
NAME | PAGE _____

_____
NAME | PAGE _____

NOTABLE CHARACTERISTICS & LIFE EVENTS: _____

_____

_____

_____

ADDITIONAL SPOUSE | PAGE_____ || ADDITIONAL CHILDREN | PAGE_____

CHARTS INCLUDED IN | PAGE _____ || APPEARS IN PHOTOS | PAGE _____ || MENTIONED IN PAGES _____

FATHER'S NAME | PAGE _____

MOTHER'S NAME | PAGE _____

NAME GIVEN AT BIRTH

_____
DATE OF BIRTH

_____
DATE OF DEATH

_____
PLACE OF BIRTH

_____
PLACE OF DEATH

_____
NAME OF SPOUSE | PAGE _____

_____
MARITAL STATUS & DATE OF MARRIAGE

_____
PLACE OF MARRIAGE

CHILDREN

_____
NAME | PAGE _____

_____
NAME | PAGE _____

_____
NAME | PAGE _____

_____
NAME | PAGE _____

_____
NAME | PAGE _____

_____
NAME | PAGE _____

_____
NAME | PAGE _____

_____
NAME | PAGE _____

_____
NAME | PAGE _____

_____
NAME | PAGE _____

NOTABLE CHARACTERISTICS & LIFE EVENTS: _____

_____

_____

_____

_____

ADDITIONAL SPOUSE | PAGE_____ || ADDITIONAL CHILDREN | PAGE_____

_____

FATHER'S NAME | PAGE _____

_____

MOTHER'S NAME | PAGE _____

_____

NAME GIVEN AT BIRTH

❖

_____

DATE OF BIRTH

_____

DATE OF DEATH

_____

PLACE OF BIRTH

_____

PLACE OF DEATH

_____

NAME OF SPOUSE | PAGE _____

_____

MARITAL STATUS & DATE OF MARRIAGE

_____

PLACE OF MARRIAGE

CHILDREN

_____

NAME | PAGE _____

_____

NAME | PAGE _____

_____

NAME | PAGE _____

_____

NAME | PAGE _____

_____

NAME | PAGE _____

_____

NAME | PAGE _____

_____

NAME | PAGE _____

_____

NAME | PAGE _____

_____

NAME | PAGE _____

_____

NAME | PAGE _____

NOTABLE CHARACTERISTICS & LIFE EVENTS: _____

_____

_____

_____

ADDITIONAL SPOUSE | PAGE_____ || ADDITIONAL CHILDREN | PAGE_____

FATHER'S NAME | PAGE _____

MOTHER'S NAME | PAGE _____

NAME GIVEN AT BIRTH

_____
DATE OF BIRTH

_____
DATE OF DEATH

_____
PLACE OF BIRTH

_____
PLACE OF DEATH

NAME OF SPOUSE | PAGE _____

_____
MARITAL STATUS & DATE OF MARRIAGE

_____
PLACE OF MARRIAGE

CHILDREN

NAME | PAGE _____

NAME | PAGE _____

NAME | PAGE _____

NAME | PAGE _____

NAME | PAGE _____

NAME | PAGE _____

NAME | PAGE _____

NAME | PAGE _____

NAME | PAGE _____

NAME | PAGE _____

NOTABLE CHARACTERISTICS & LIFE EVENTS: _____

_____

_____

_____

ADDITIONAL SPOUSE | PAGE_____ || ADDITIONAL CHILDREN | PAGE_____

CHARTS INCLUDED IN | PAGE _____ || APPEARS IN PHOTOS | PAGE _____ || MENTIONED IN PAGES _____

FATHER'S NAME | PAGE _____

MOTHER'S NAME | PAGE _____

NAME GIVEN AT BIRTH

_____
DATE OF BIRTH

_____
DATE OF DEATH

_____
PLACE OF BIRTH

_____
PLACE OF DEATH

_____
NAME OF SPOUSE | PAGE _____

_____
MARITAL STATUS & DATE OF MARRIAGE

_____
PLACE OF MARRIAGE

CHILDREN

NAME | PAGE _____

NAME | PAGE _____

NAME | PAGE _____

NAME | PAGE _____

NAME | PAGE _____

NAME | PAGE _____

NAME | PAGE _____

NAME | PAGE _____

NAME | PAGE _____

NAME | PAGE _____

NOTABLE CHARACTERISTICS & LIFE EVENTS:

_____

_____

_____

_____

ADDITIONAL SPOUSE | PAGE _____ || ADDITIONAL CHILDREN | PAGE _____

CHARTS INCLUDED IN | PAGE _____ || APPEARS IN PHOTOS | PAGE _____ || MENTIONED IN PAGES _____

_____ _____
FATHER'S NAME | PAGE _____   MOTHER'S NAME | PAGE _____

NAME GIVEN AT BIRTH

_____   _____
DATE OF BIRTH   DATE OF DEATH

_____   _____
PLACE OF BIRTH   PLACE OF DEATH

_____
NAME OF SPOUSE | PAGE_____

_____ _____
MARITAL STATUS & DATE OF MARRIAGE   PLACE OF MARRIAGE

CHILDREN

_____ _____
NAME | PAGE _____   NAME | PAGE _____

_____ _____
NAME | PAGE _____   NAME | PAGE _____

_____ _____
NAME | PAGE _____   NAME | PAGE _____

_____ _____
NAME | PAGE _____   NAME | PAGE _____

_____ _____
NAME | PAGE _____   NAME | PAGE _____

NOTABLE CHARACTERISTICS & LIFE EVENTS: _____

_____

_____

_____

ADDITIONAL SPOUSE | PAGE_____ || ADDITIONAL CHILDREN | PAGE_____

_____

FATHER'S NAME | PAGE _____

_____

MOTHER'S NAME | PAGE _____

NAME GIVEN AT BIRTH

_____

DATE OF BIRTH

_____

DATE OF DEATH

_____

PLACE OF BIRTH

_____

PLACE OF DEATH

_____

NAME OF SPOUSE | PAGE _____

_____

MARITAL STATUS & DATE OF MARRIAGE

_____

PLACE OF MARRIAGE

CHILDREN

_____

NAME | PAGE _____

_____

NAME | PAGE _____

_____

NAME | PAGE _____

_____

NAME | PAGE _____

_____

NAME | PAGE _____

_____

NAME | PAGE _____

_____

NAME | PAGE _____

_____

NAME | PAGE _____

_____

NAME | PAGE _____

_____

NAME | PAGE _____

NOTABLE CHARACTERISTICS & LIFE EVENTS:

_____

_____

_____

_____

ADDITIONAL SPOUSE | PAGE _____ || ADDITIONAL CHILDREN | PAGE _____

_____
FATHER'S NAME | PAGE _____

_____
MOTHER'S NAME | PAGE _____

NAME GIVEN AT BIRTH

_____
DATE OF BIRTH

_____
DATE OF DEATH

_____
PLACE OF BIRTH

_____
PLACE OF DEATH

_____
NAME OF SPOUSE | PAGE_____

_____
MARITAL STATUS & DATE OF MARRIAGE

_____
PLACE OF MARRIAGE

CHILDREN

_____
NAME | PAGE _____

_____
NAME | PAGE _____

_____
NAME | PAGE _____

_____
NAME | PAGE _____

_____
NAME | PAGE _____

_____
NAME | PAGE _____

_____
NAME | PAGE _____

_____
NAME | PAGE _____

_____
NAME | PAGE _____

_____
NAME | PAGE _____

NOTABLE CHARACTERISTICS & LIFE EVENTS:
_____
_____
_____
_____

ADDITIONAL SPOUSE | PAGE_____ || ADDITIONAL CHILDREN | PAGE_____

CHARTS INCLUDED IN | PAGE _____ || APPEARS IN PHOTOS | PAGE _____ || MENTIONED IN PAGES _____

FATHER'S NAME | PAGE _____   MOTHER'S NAME | PAGE _____

NAME GIVEN AT BIRTH

_____
DATE OF BIRTH

_____
PLACE OF BIRTH

_____
DATE OF DEATH

_____
PLACE OF DEATH

_____
NAME OF SPOUSE | PAGE_____

_____
MARITAL STATUS & DATE OF MARRIAGE

_____
PLACE OF MARRIAGE

CHILDREN

_____
NAME | PAGE _____

_____
NAME | PAGE _____

_____
NAME | PAGE _____

_____
NAME | PAGE _____

_____
NAME | PAGE _____

_____
NAME | PAGE _____

_____
NAME | PAGE _____

_____
NAME | PAGE _____

_____
NAME | PAGE _____

_____
NAME | PAGE _____

NOTABLE CHARACTERISTICS & LIFE EVENTS:

_____
_____
_____
_____

ADDITIONAL SPOUSE | PAGE_____ || ADDITIONAL CHILDREN | PAGE_____

CHARTS INCLUDED IN | PAGE _____ || APPEARS IN PHOTOS | PAGE _____ || MENTIONED IN PAGES _____

_____

FATHER'S NAME | PAGE _____

_____

MOTHER'S NAME | PAGE _____

_____

NAME GIVEN AT BIRTH

_____

DATE OF BIRTH

_____

DATE OF DEATH

_____

PLACE OF BIRTH

_____

PLACE OF DEATH

_____

NAME OF SPOUSE | PAGE_____

_____

MARITAL STATUS & DATE OF MARRIAGE

_____

PLACE OF MARRIAGE

CHILDREN

_____

NAME | PAGE _____

_____

NAME | PAGE _____

_____

NAME | PAGE _____

_____

NAME | PAGE _____

_____

NAME | PAGE _____

_____

NAME | PAGE _____

_____

NAME | PAGE _____

_____

NAME | PAGE _____

_____

NAME | PAGE _____

_____

NAME | PAGE _____

NOTABLE CHARACTERISTICS & LIFE EVENTS:

_____

_____

_____

_____

ADDITIONAL SPOUSE | PAGE_____ || ADDITIONAL CHILDREN | PAGE_____

CHARTS INCLUDED IN | PAGE _____ || APPEARS IN PHOTOS | PAGE _____ || MENTIONED IN PAGES _____

FATHER'S NAME | PAGE _____

MOTHER'S NAME | PAGE _____

NAME GIVEN AT BIRTH

DATE OF BIRTH

DATE OF DEATH

PLACE OF BIRTH

PLACE OF DEATH

NAME OF SPOUSE | PAGE_____

MARITAL STATUS & DATE OF MARRIAGE

PLACE OF MARRIAGE

CHILDREN

NAME | PAGE _____

NAME | PAGE _____

NAME | PAGE _____

NAME | PAGE _____

NAME | PAGE _____

NAME | PAGE _____

NAME | PAGE _____

NAME | PAGE _____

NAME | PAGE _____

NAME | PAGE _____

NOTABLE CHARACTERISTICS & LIFE EVENTS:

ADDITIONAL SPOUSE | PAGE_____ || ADDITIONAL CHILDREN | PAGE_____

_____

FATHER'S NAME | PAGE _____

_____

MOTHER'S NAME | PAGE _____

_____

NAME GIVEN AT BIRTH

_____

DATE OF BIRTH

_____

DATE OF DEATH

_____

PLACE OF BIRTH

_____

PLACE OF DEATH

_____

NAME OF SPOUSE | PAGE _____

_____

MARITAL STATUS & DATE OF MARRIAGE

_____

PLACE OF MARRIAGE

CHILDREN

_____

NAME | PAGE _____

_____

NAME | PAGE _____

_____

NAME | PAGE _____

_____

NAME | PAGE _____

_____

NAME | PAGE _____

_____

NAME | PAGE _____

_____

NAME | PAGE _____

_____

NAME | PAGE _____

_____

NAME | PAGE _____

_____

NAME | PAGE _____

NOTABLE CHARACTERISTICS & LIFE EVENTS:

_____

_____

_____

_____

ADDITIONAL SPOUSE | PAGE _____ || ADDITIONAL CHILDREN | PAGE _____

CHARTS INCLUDED IN | PAGE _____ || APPEARS IN PHOTOS | PAGE _____ || MENTIONED IN PAGES _____

FATHER'S NAME | PAGE _____

MOTHER'S NAME | PAGE _____

NAME GIVEN AT BIRTH

_____
DATE OF BIRTH

_____
DATE OF DEATH

_____
PLACE OF BIRTH

_____
PLACE OF DEATH

_____
NAME OF SPOUSE | PAGE _____

_____
MARITAL STATUS & DATE OF MARRIAGE

_____
PLACE OF MARRIAGE

CHILDREN

_____
NAME | PAGE _____

_____
NAME | PAGE _____

_____
NAME | PAGE _____

_____
NAME | PAGE _____

_____
NAME | PAGE _____

_____
NAME | PAGE _____

_____
NAME | PAGE _____

_____
NAME | PAGE _____

_____
NAME | PAGE _____

_____
NAME | PAGE _____

NOTABLE CHARACTERISTICS & LIFE EVENTS: _____
_____
_____
_____
_____

ADDITIONAL SPOUSE | PAGE_____ || ADDITIONAL CHILDREN | PAGE_____

_____

FATHER'S NAME | PAGE _____

_____

MOTHER'S NAME | PAGE _____

_____

NAME GIVEN AT BIRTH

_____
DATE OF BIRTH

_____
DATE OF DEATH

_____
PLACE OF BIRTH

_____
PLACE OF DEATH

_____
NAME OF SPOUSE | PAGE _____

_____
MARITAL STATUS & DATE OF MARRIAGE

_____
PLACE OF MARRIAGE

CHILDREN

_____
NAME | PAGE _____

_____
NAME | PAGE _____

_____
NAME | PAGE _____

_____
NAME | PAGE _____

_____
NAME | PAGE _____

_____
NAME | PAGE _____

_____
NAME | PAGE _____

_____
NAME | PAGE _____

_____
NAME | PAGE _____

_____
NAME | PAGE _____

NOTABLE CHARACTERISTICS & LIFE EVENTS: _____

_____

_____

_____

ADDITIONAL SPOUSE | PAGE _____ || ADDITIONAL CHILDREN | PAGE _____

CHARTS INCLUDED IN | PAGE _____ || APPEARS IN PHOTOS | PAGE _____ || MENTIONED IN PAGES _____

_____   _____
FATHER'S NAME | PAGE _____   MOTHER'S NAME | PAGE _____

_____
NAME GIVEN AT BIRTH

_____
DATE OF BIRTH

_____
DATE OF DEATH

_____
PLACE OF BIRTH

_____
PLACE OF DEATH

_____
NAME OF SPOUSE | PAGE_____

_____   _____
MARITAL STATUS & DATE OF MARRIAGE   PLACE OF MARRIAGE

CHILDREN

_____   _____
NAME | PAGE _____   NAME | PAGE _____

_____   _____
NAME | PAGE _____   NAME | PAGE _____

_____   _____
NAME | PAGE _____   NAME | PAGE _____

_____   _____
NAME | PAGE _____   NAME | PAGE _____

_____   _____
NAME | PAGE _____   NAME | PAGE _____

NOTABLE CHARACTERISTICS & LIFE EVENTS:

_____

_____

_____

_____

ADDITIONAL SPOUSE | PAGE_____ || ADDITIONAL CHILDREN | PAGE_____

CHARTS INCLUDED IN | PAGE _____ || APPEARS IN PHOTOS | PAGE _____ || MENTIONED IN PAGES _____

_____

FATHER'S NAME | PAGE _____

_____

MOTHER'S NAME | PAGE _____

_____

NAME GIVEN AT BIRTH

_____
DATE OF BIRTH

_____
DATE OF DEATH

_____
PLACE OF BIRTH

_____
PLACE OF DEATH

_____
NAME OF SPOUSE | PAGE_____

_____
MARITAL STATUS & DATE OF MARRIAGE

_____
PLACE OF MARRIAGE

CHILDREN

_____
NAME | PAGE _____

_____
NAME | PAGE _____

_____
NAME | PAGE _____

_____
NAME | PAGE _____

_____
NAME | PAGE _____

_____
NAME | PAGE _____

_____
NAME | PAGE _____

_____
NAME | PAGE _____

_____
NAME | PAGE _____

_____
NAME | PAGE _____

NOTABLE CHARACTERISTICS & LIFE EVENTS: _____

_____

_____

_____

ADDITIONAL SPOUSE | PAGE_____ || ADDITIONAL CHILDREN | PAGE_____

CHARTS INCLUDED IN | PAGE _____ || APPEARS IN PHOTOS | PAGE _____ || MENTIONED IN PAGES _____

_____

FATHER'S NAME | PAGE _____

_____

MOTHER'S NAME | PAGE _____

_____

NAME GIVEN AT BIRTH

_____
DATE OF BIRTH

_____
PLACE OF BIRTH

_____
DATE OF DEATH

_____
PLACE OF DEATH

_____
NAME OF SPOUSE | PAGE_____

_____
MARITAL STATUS & DATE OF MARRIAGE

_____
PLACE OF MARRIAGE

CHILDREN

_____
NAME | PAGE _____

_____
NAME | PAGE _____

_____
NAME | PAGE _____

_____
NAME | PAGE _____

_____
NAME | PAGE _____

_____
NAME | PAGE _____

_____
NAME | PAGE _____

_____
NAME | PAGE _____

_____
NAME | PAGE _____

_____
NAME | PAGE _____

NOTABLE CHARACTERISTICS & LIFE EVENTS: _____

_____

_____

_____

ADDITIONAL SPOUSE | PAGE_____ || ADDITIONAL CHILDREN | PAGE_____

CHARTS INCLUDED IN | PAGE _____ || APPEARS IN PHOTOS | PAGE _____ || MENTIONED IN PAGES _____

FATHER'S NAME | PAGE _____

MOTHER'S NAME | PAGE _____

NAME GIVEN AT BIRTH

_____
DATE OF BIRTH

_____
DATE OF DEATH

_____
PLACE OF BIRTH

_____
PLACE OF DEATH

_____
NAME OF SPOUSE | PAGE_____

_____
MARITAL STATUS & DATE OF MARRIAGE

_____
PLACE OF MARRIAGE

CHILDREN

_____
NAME | PAGE _____

_____
NAME | PAGE _____

_____
NAME | PAGE _____

_____
NAME | PAGE _____

_____
NAME | PAGE _____

_____
NAME | PAGE _____

_____
NAME | PAGE _____

_____
NAME | PAGE _____

_____
NAME | PAGE _____

_____
NAME | PAGE _____

NOTABLE CHARACTERISTICS & LIFE EVENTS:

_____

_____

_____

_____

ADDITIONAL SPOUSE | PAGE_____ || ADDITIONAL CHILDREN | PAGE_____

CHARTS INCLUDED IN | PAGE _____ || APPEARS IN PHOTOS | PAGE _____ || MENTIONED IN PAGES _____

FATHER'S NAME | PAGE _____

MOTHER'S NAME | PAGE _____

NAME GIVEN AT BIRTH

DATE OF BIRTH

DATE OF DEATH

PLACE OF BIRTH

PLACE OF DEATH

NAME OF SPOUSE | PAGE_____

MARITAL STATUS & DATE OF MARRIAGE

PLACE OF MARRIAGE

CHILDREN

NAME | PAGE _____

NAME | PAGE _____

NAME | PAGE _____

NAME | PAGE _____

NAME | PAGE _____

NAME | PAGE _____

NAME | PAGE _____

NAME | PAGE _____

NAME | PAGE _____

NAME | PAGE _____

NOTABLE CHARACTERISTICS & LIFE EVENTS: _____

_____

_____

_____

ADDITIONAL SPOUSE | PAGE_____ || ADDITIONAL CHILDREN | PAGE_____

_____
FATHER'S NAME | PAGE _____

_____
MOTHER'S NAME | PAGE _____

_____

NAME GIVEN AT BIRTH

_____
DATE OF BIRTH

_____
DATE OF DEATH

_____
PLACE OF BIRTH

_____
PLACE OF DEATH

_____
NAME OF SPOUSE | PAGE_____

_____
MARITAL STATUS & DATE OF MARRIAGE

_____
PLACE OF MARRIAGE

CHILDREN

_____
NAME | PAGE _____

_____
NAME | PAGE _____

_____
NAME | PAGE _____

_____
NAME | PAGE _____

_____
NAME | PAGE _____

_____
NAME | PAGE _____

_____
NAME | PAGE _____

_____
NAME | PAGE _____

_____
NAME | PAGE _____

_____
NAME | PAGE _____

NOTABLE CHARACTERISTICS & LIFE EVENTS:
_____
_____
_____
_____

ADDITIONAL SPOUSE | PAGE_____ || ADDITIONAL CHILDREN | PAGE_____

CHARTS INCLUDED IN | PAGE _____ || APPEARS IN PHOTOS | PAGE _____ || MENTIONED IN PAGES _____

FATHER'S NAME | PAGE _____

MOTHER'S NAME | PAGE _____

NAME GIVEN AT BIRTH

_____
DATE OF BIRTH

_____
DATE OF DEATH

_____
PLACE OF BIRTH

_____
PLACE OF DEATH

_____
NAME OF SPOUSE | PAGE _____

_____
MARITAL STATUS & DATE OF MARRIAGE

_____
PLACE OF MARRIAGE

CHILDREN

_____
NAME | PAGE _____

_____
NAME | PAGE _____

_____
NAME | PAGE _____

_____
NAME | PAGE _____

_____
NAME | PAGE _____

_____
NAME | PAGE _____

_____
NAME | PAGE _____

_____
NAME | PAGE _____

_____
NAME | PAGE _____

_____
NAME | PAGE _____

NOTABLE CHARACTERISTICS & LIFE EVENTS:

_____

_____

_____

_____

ADDITIONAL SPOUSE | PAGE _____ || ADDITIONAL CHILDREN | PAGE _____

CHARTS INCLUDED IN | PAGE _____ || APPEARS IN PHOTOS | PAGE _____ || MENTIONED IN PAGES _____

FATHER'S NAME | PAGE _____

MOTHER'S NAME | PAGE _____

NAME GIVEN AT BIRTH

_____

DATE OF BIRTH

_____

DATE OF DEATH

_____

PLACE OF BIRTH

_____

PLACE OF DEATH

_____

NAME OF SPOUSE | PAGE_____

_____

MARITAL STATUS & DATE OF MARRIAGE

_____

PLACE OF MARRIAGE

CHILDREN

_____

NAME | PAGE _____

_____

NAME | PAGE _____

_____

NAME | PAGE _____

_____

NAME | PAGE _____

_____

NAME | PAGE _____

_____

NAME | PAGE _____

_____

NAME | PAGE _____

_____

NAME | PAGE _____

_____

NAME | PAGE _____

_____

NAME | PAGE _____

NOTABLE CHARACTERISTICS & LIFE EVENTS: _____

_____

_____

_____

ADDITIONAL SPOUSE | PAGE_____ || ADDITIONAL CHILDREN | PAGE_____

_____

FATHER'S NAME | PAGE _____

_____

MOTHER'S NAME | PAGE _____

_____

NAME GIVEN AT BIRTH

_____
DATE OF BIRTH

_____
DATE OF DEATH

_____
PLACE OF BIRTH

_____
PLACE OF DEATH

_____
NAME OF SPOUSE | PAGE_____

_____
MARITAL STATUS & DATE OF MARRIAGE

_____
PLACE OF MARRIAGE

CHILDREN

_____
NAME | PAGE _____

_____
NAME | PAGE _____

_____
NAME | PAGE _____

_____
NAME | PAGE _____

_____
NAME | PAGE _____

_____
NAME | PAGE _____

_____
NAME | PAGE _____

_____
NAME | PAGE _____

_____
NAME | PAGE _____

_____
NAME | PAGE _____

NOTABLE CHARACTERISTICS & LIFE EVENTS: _____

_____

_____

_____

ADDITIONAL SPOUSE | PAGE_____ || ADDITIONAL CHILDREN | PAGE_____

_____
FATHER'S NAME | PAGE _____

_____
MOTHER'S NAME | PAGE _____

_____

NAME GIVEN AT BIRTH

_____
DATE OF BIRTH

_____
DATE OF DEATH

_____
PLACE OF BIRTH

_____
PLACE OF DEATH

_____
NAME OF SPOUSE | PAGE_____

_____
MARITAL STATUS & DATE OF MARRIAGE

_____
PLACE OF MARRIAGE

CHILDREN

_____
NAME | PAGE _____

_____
NAME | PAGE _____

_____
NAME | PAGE _____

_____
NAME | PAGE _____

_____
NAME | PAGE _____

_____
NAME | PAGE _____

_____
NAME | PAGE _____

_____
NAME | PAGE _____

_____
NAME | PAGE _____

_____
NAME | PAGE _____

NOTABLE CHARACTERISTICS & LIFE EVENTS: _____
_____
_____
_____

ADDITIONAL SPOUSE | PAGE_____ || ADDITIONAL CHILDREN | PAGE_____

FATHER'S NAME | PAGE _____

MOTHER'S NAME | PAGE _____

NAME GIVEN AT BIRTH

_____
DATE OF BIRTH

_____
DATE OF DEATH

_____
PLACE OF BIRTH

_____
PLACE OF DEATH

_____
NAME OF SPOUSE | PAGE _____

_____
MARITAL STATUS & DATE OF MARRIAGE

_____
PLACE OF MARRIAGE

CHILDREN

_____
NAME | PAGE _____

_____
NAME | PAGE _____

_____
NAME | PAGE _____

_____
NAME | PAGE _____

_____
NAME | PAGE _____

_____
NAME | PAGE _____

_____
NAME | PAGE _____

_____
NAME | PAGE _____

_____
NAME | PAGE _____

_____
NAME | PAGE _____

NOTABLE CHARACTERISTICS & LIFE EVENTS: _____

_____

_____

_____

ADDITIONAL SPOUSE | PAGE_____ || ADDITIONAL CHILDREN | PAGE_____

CHARTS INCLUDED IN | PAGE _____ || APPEARS IN PHOTOS | PAGE _____ || MENTIONED IN PAGES _____

FATHER'S NAME | PAGE _____

MOTHER'S NAME | PAGE _____

NAME GIVEN AT BIRTH

_____

DATE OF BIRTH

_____

DATE OF DEATH

_____

PLACE OF BIRTH

_____

PLACE OF DEATH

NAME OF SPOUSE | PAGE_____

_____

MARITAL STATUS & DATE OF MARRIAGE

PLACE OF MARRIAGE

CHILDREN

NAME | PAGE _____

NAME | PAGE _____

NAME | PAGE _____

NAME | PAGE _____

NAME | PAGE _____

NAME | PAGE _____

NAME | PAGE _____

NAME | PAGE _____

NAME | PAGE _____

NAME | PAGE _____

NOTABLE CHARACTERISTICS & LIFE EVENTS:

_____

_____

_____

_____

ADDITIONAL SPOUSE | PAGE_____ || ADDITIONAL CHILDREN | PAGE_____

CHARTS INCLUDED IN | PAGE _____ || APPEARS IN PHOTOS | PAGE _____ || MENTIONED IN PAGES _____

FATHER'S NAME | PAGE _____

MOTHER'S NAME | PAGE _____

NAME GIVEN AT BIRTH

_____
DATE OF BIRTH

_____
DATE OF DEATH

_____
PLACE OF BIRTH

_____
PLACE OF DEATH

_____
NAME OF SPOUSE | PAGE_____

_____
MARITAL STATUS & DATE OF MARRIAGE

_____
PLACE OF MARRIAGE

CHILDREN

_____
NAME | PAGE _____

_____
NAME | PAGE _____

_____
NAME | PAGE _____

_____
NAME | PAGE _____

_____
NAME | PAGE _____

_____
NAME | PAGE _____

_____
NAME | PAGE _____

_____
NAME | PAGE _____

_____
NAME | PAGE _____

_____
NAME | PAGE _____

NOTABLE CHARACTERISTICS & LIFE EVENTS:

_____

_____

_____

_____

ADDITIONAL SPOUSE | PAGE_____ || ADDITIONAL CHILDREN | PAGE_____

_____
FATHER'S NAME | PAGE _____

_____
MOTHER'S NAME | PAGE _____

_____

NAME GIVEN AT BIRTH

_____
DATE OF BIRTH

_____
DATE OF DEATH

_____
PLACE OF BIRTH

_____
PLACE OF DEATH

_____
NAME OF SPOUSE | PAGE_____

_____
MARITAL STATUS & DATE OF MARRIAGE

_____
PLACE OF MARRIAGE

CHILDREN

_____
NAME | PAGE _____

_____
NAME | PAGE _____

_____
NAME | PAGE _____

_____
NAME | PAGE _____

_____
NAME | PAGE _____

_____
NAME | PAGE _____

_____
NAME | PAGE _____

_____
NAME | PAGE _____

_____
NAME | PAGE _____

_____
NAME | PAGE _____

NOTABLE CHARACTERISTICS & LIFE EVENTS:

_____

_____

_____

_____

_____
FATHER'S NAME | PAGE _____

_____
MOTHER'S NAME | PAGE _____

_____

NAME GIVEN AT BIRTH

_____
DATE OF BIRTH

_____
DATE OF DEATH

_____
PLACE OF BIRTH

_____
PLACE OF DEATH

_____
NAME OF SPOUSE | PAGE_____

_____
MARITAL STATUS & DATE OF MARRIAGE

_____
PLACE OF MARRIAGE

CHILDREN

_____
NAME | PAGE _____

_____
NAME | PAGE _____

_____
NAME | PAGE _____

_____
NAME | PAGE _____

_____
NAME | PAGE _____

_____
NAME | PAGE _____

_____
NAME | PAGE _____

_____
NAME | PAGE _____

_____
NAME | PAGE _____

_____
NAME | PAGE _____

NOTABLE CHARACTERISTICS & LIFE EVENTS: _____

_____

_____

_____

ADDITIONAL SPOUSE | PAGE_____ || ADDITIONAL CHILDREN | PAGE_____

CHARTS INCLUDED IN | PAGE _____ || APPEARS IN PHOTOS | PAGE _____ || MENTIONED IN PAGES _____

_____

FATHER'S NAME | PAGE _____

_____

MOTHER'S NAME | PAGE _____

_____

NAME GIVEN AT BIRTH

_____
DATE OF BIRTH

_____
DATE OF DEATH

_____
PLACE OF BIRTH

_____
PLACE OF DEATH

_____
NAME OF SPOUSE | PAGE _____

_____
MARITAL STATUS & DATE OF MARRIAGE

_____
PLACE OF MARRIAGE

CHILDREN

_____
NAME | PAGE _____

_____
NAME | PAGE _____

_____
NAME | PAGE _____

_____
NAME | PAGE _____

_____
NAME | PAGE _____

_____
NAME | PAGE _____

_____
NAME | PAGE _____

_____
NAME | PAGE _____

_____
NAME | PAGE _____

_____
NAME | PAGE _____

NOTABLE CHARACTERISTICS & LIFE EVENTS: _____

_____

_____

_____

ADDITIONAL SPOUSE | PAGE_____ || ADDITIONAL CHILDREN | PAGE_____

CHARTS INCLUDED IN | PAGE _____ || APPEARS IN PHOTOS | PAGE _____ || MENTIONED IN PAGES _____

_____ | _____

FATHER'S NAME | PAGE _____ | MOTHER'S NAME | PAGE _____

_____

NAME GIVEN AT BIRTH

_____ | _____

DATE OF BIRTH | DATE OF DEATH

_____ | _____

PLACE OF BIRTH | PLACE OF DEATH

_____

NAME OF SPOUSE | PAGE_____

_____ | _____

MARITAL STATUS & DATE OF MARRIAGE | PLACE OF MARRIAGE

CHILDREN

_____ | _____
NAME | PAGE _____ | NAME | PAGE _____

_____ | _____
NAME | PAGE _____ | NAME | PAGE _____

_____ | _____
NAME | PAGE _____ | NAME | PAGE _____

_____ | _____
NAME | PAGE _____ | NAME | PAGE _____

_____ | _____
NAME | PAGE _____ | NAME | PAGE _____

NOTABLE CHARACTERISTICS & LIFE EVENTS: _____

_____

_____

_____

ADDITIONAL SPOUSE | PAGE_____ || ADDITIONAL CHILDREN | PAGE_____

FATHER'S NAME | PAGE _____

MOTHER'S NAME | PAGE _____

NAME GIVEN AT BIRTH

_____
DATE OF BIRTH

_____
DATE OF DEATH

_____
PLACE OF BIRTH

_____
PLACE OF DEATH

_____
NAME OF SPOUSE | PAGE _____

_____
MARITAL STATUS & DATE OF MARRIAGE

_____
PLACE OF MARRIAGE

CHILDREN

_____
NAME | PAGE _____

_____
NAME | PAGE _____

_____
NAME | PAGE _____

_____
NAME | PAGE _____

_____
NAME | PAGE _____

_____
NAME | PAGE _____

_____
NAME | PAGE _____

_____
NAME | PAGE _____

_____
NAME | PAGE _____

_____
NAME | PAGE _____

NOTABLE CHARACTERISTICS & LIFE EVENTS: _____

_____

_____

_____

ADDITIONAL SPOUSE | PAGE _____ || ADDITIONAL CHILDREN | PAGE _____

CHARTS INCLUDED IN | PAGE _____ || APPEARS IN PHOTOS | PAGE _____ || MENTIONED IN PAGES _____

FATHER'S NAME | PAGE _____

MOTHER'S NAME | PAGE _____

NAME GIVEN AT BIRTH

_____
DATE OF BIRTH

_____
DATE OF DEATH

_____
PLACE OF BIRTH

_____
PLACE OF DEATH

_____
NAME OF SPOUSE | PAGE _____

_____
MARITAL STATUS & DATE OF MARRIAGE

_____
PLACE OF MARRIAGE

CHILDREN

_____
NAME | PAGE _____

_____
NAME | PAGE _____

_____
NAME | PAGE _____

_____
NAME | PAGE _____

_____
NAME | PAGE _____

_____
NAME | PAGE _____

_____
NAME | PAGE _____

_____
NAME | PAGE _____

_____
NAME | PAGE _____

_____
NAME | PAGE _____

NOTABLE CHARACTERISTICS & LIFE EVENTS:

_____

_____

_____

_____

ADDITIONAL SPOUSE | PAGE _____ || ADDITIONAL CHILDREN | PAGE _____

_____

FATHER'S NAME | PAGE _____

_____

MOTHER'S NAME | PAGE _____

_____

NAME GIVEN AT BIRTH

_____

DATE OF BIRTH

_____

DATE OF DEATH

_____

PLACE OF BIRTH

_____

PLACE OF DEATH

_____

NAME OF SPOUSE | PAGE _____

_____   _____

MARITAL STATUS & DATE OF MARRIAGE   PLACE OF MARRIAGE

CHILDREN

_____   _____

NAME | PAGE _____   NAME | PAGE _____

_____   _____

NAME | PAGE _____   NAME | PAGE _____

_____   _____

NAME | PAGE _____   NAME | PAGE _____

_____   _____

NAME | PAGE _____   NAME | PAGE _____

_____   _____

NAME | PAGE _____   NAME | PAGE _____

NOTABLE CHARACTERISTICS & LIFE EVENTS: _____

_____

_____

_____

ADDITIONAL SPOUSE | PAGE_____ || ADDITIONAL CHILDREN | PAGE_____

CHARTS INCLUDED IN | PAGE _____ || APPEARS IN PHOTOS | PAGE _____ || MENTIONED IN PAGES _____

_____ | _____

FATHER'S NAME | PAGE _____   MOTHER'S NAME | PAGE _____

_____

NAME GIVEN AT BIRTH

_____   _____

DATE OF BIRTH   DATE OF DEATH

_____   _____

PLACE OF BIRTH   PLACE OF DEATH

_____

NAME OF SPOUSE | PAGE_____

_____   _____

MARITAL STATUS & DATE OF MARRIAGE   PLACE OF MARRIAGE

CHILDREN

NAME | PAGE _____   NAME | PAGE _____

NAME | PAGE _____   NAME | PAGE _____

NAME | PAGE _____   NAME | PAGE _____

NAME | PAGE _____   NAME | PAGE _____

NAME | PAGE _____   NAME | PAGE _____

NOTABLE CHARACTERISTICS & LIFE EVENTS: _____

_____

_____

_____

ADDITIONAL SPOUSE | PAGE_____ || ADDITIONAL CHILDREN | PAGE_____

_____
FATHER'S NAME | PAGE _____

_____
MOTHER'S NAME | PAGE _____

_____

NAME GIVEN AT BIRTH

_____
DATE OF BIRTH

_____
DATE OF DEATH

_____
PLACE OF BIRTH

_____
PLACE OF DEATH

_____
NAME OF SPOUSE | PAGE_____

_____
MARITAL STATUS & DATE OF MARRIAGE

_____
PLACE OF MARRIAGE

CHILDREN

_____
NAME | PAGE _____

_____
NAME | PAGE _____

_____
NAME | PAGE _____

_____
NAME | PAGE _____

_____
NAME | PAGE _____

_____
NAME | PAGE _____

_____
NAME | PAGE _____

_____
NAME | PAGE _____

_____
NAME | PAGE _____

_____
NAME | PAGE _____

NOTABLE CHARACTERISTICS & LIFE EVENTS:
_____
_____
_____
_____

ADDITIONAL SPOUSE | PAGE_____ || ADDITIONAL CHILDREN | PAGE_____

CHARTS INCLUDED IN | PAGE _____ || APPEARS IN PHOTOS | PAGE _____ || MENTIONED IN PAGES _____

_____

FATHER'S NAME | PAGE _____

_____

MOTHER'S NAME | PAGE _____

_____

NAME GIVEN AT BIRTH

_____
DATE OF BIRTH

_____
DATE OF DEATH

_____
PLACE OF BIRTH

_____
PLACE OF DEATH

_____
NAME OF SPOUSE | PAGE_____

_____
MARITAL STATUS & DATE OF MARRIAGE

_____
PLACE OF MARRIAGE

CHILDREN

_____
NAME | PAGE _____

_____
NAME | PAGE _____

_____
NAME | PAGE _____

_____
NAME | PAGE _____

_____
NAME | PAGE _____

_____
NAME | PAGE _____

_____
NAME | PAGE _____

_____
NAME | PAGE _____

_____
NAME | PAGE _____

_____
NAME | PAGE _____

NOTABLE CHARACTERISTICS & LIFE EVENTS:

_____

_____

_____

_____

ADDITIONAL SPOUSE | PAGE_____ || ADDITIONAL CHILDREN | PAGE_____

CHARTS INCLUDED IN | PAGE _____ || APPEARS IN PHOTOS | PAGE _____ || MENTIONED IN PAGES _____

FATHER'S NAME | PAGE _____

MOTHER'S NAME | PAGE _____

NAME GIVEN AT BIRTH

_____
DATE OF BIRTH

_____
DATE OF DEATH

_____
PLACE OF BIRTH

_____
PLACE OF DEATH

NAME OF SPOUSE | PAGE_____

_____
MARITAL STATUS & DATE OF MARRIAGE

_____
PLACE OF MARRIAGE

CHILDREN

NAME | PAGE _____

NAME | PAGE _____

NAME | PAGE _____

NAME | PAGE _____

NAME | PAGE _____

NAME | PAGE _____

NAME | PAGE _____

NAME | PAGE _____

NAME | PAGE _____

NAME | PAGE _____

NOTABLE CHARACTERISTICS & LIFE EVENTS:

ADDITIONAL SPOUSE | PAGE_____ || ADDITIONAL CHILDREN | PAGE_____

_____

FATHER'S NAME | PAGE _____

_____

MOTHER'S NAME | PAGE _____

_____

NAME GIVEN AT BIRTH

_____
DATE OF BIRTH

_____
PLACE OF BIRTH

_____
DATE OF DEATH

_____
PLACE OF DEATH

_____
NAME OF SPOUSE | PAGE _____

_____
MARITAL STATUS & DATE OF MARRIAGE

_____
PLACE OF MARRIAGE

CHILDREN

_____
NAME | PAGE _____

_____
NAME | PAGE _____

_____
NAME | PAGE _____

_____
NAME | PAGE _____

_____
NAME | PAGE _____

_____
NAME | PAGE _____

_____
NAME | PAGE _____

_____
NAME | PAGE _____

_____
NAME | PAGE _____

_____
NAME | PAGE _____

NOTABLE CHARACTERISTICS & LIFE EVENTS:

_____

_____

_____

_____

ADDITIONAL SPOUSE | PAGE_____ || ADDITIONAL CHILDREN | PAGE_____

CHARTS INCLUDED IN | PAGE _____ || APPEARS IN PHOTOS | PAGE _____ || MENTIONED IN PAGES _____

FATHER'S NAME | PAGE _____

MOTHER'S NAME | PAGE _____

NAME GIVEN AT BIRTH

_____
DATE OF BIRTH

_____
DATE OF DEATH

_____
PLACE OF BIRTH

_____
PLACE OF DEATH

_____
NAME OF SPOUSE | PAGE_____

_____
MARITAL STATUS & DATE OF MARRIAGE

_____
PLACE OF MARRIAGE

CHILDREN

_____
NAME | PAGE _____

_____
NAME | PAGE _____

_____
NAME | PAGE _____

_____
NAME | PAGE _____

_____
NAME | PAGE _____

_____
NAME | PAGE _____

_____
NAME | PAGE _____

_____
NAME | PAGE _____

_____
NAME | PAGE _____

_____
NAME | PAGE _____

NOTABLE CHARACTERISTICS & LIFE EVENTS:

_____
_____
_____
_____

ADDITIONAL SPOUSE | PAGE_____ || ADDITIONAL CHILDREN | PAGE_____

CHARTS INCLUDED IN | PAGE _____ || APPEARS IN PHOTOS | PAGE _____ || MENTIONED IN PAGES _____

FATHER'S NAME | PAGE _____   MOTHER'S NAME | PAGE _____

NAME GIVEN AT BIRTH

_____   _____
DATE OF BIRTH   DATE OF DEATH

_____   _____
PLACE OF BIRTH   PLACE OF DEATH

_____
NAME OF SPOUSE | PAGE _____

_____   _____
MARITAL STATUS & DATE OF MARRIAGE   PLACE OF MARRIAGE

CHILDREN

_____   _____
NAME | PAGE _____   NAME | PAGE _____

_____   _____
NAME | PAGE _____   NAME | PAGE _____

_____   _____
NAME | PAGE _____   NAME | PAGE _____

_____   _____
NAME | PAGE _____   NAME | PAGE _____

_____   _____
NAME | PAGE _____   NAME | PAGE _____

NOTABLE CHARACTERISTICS & LIFE EVENTS:
_____
_____
_____
_____

ADDITIONAL SPOUSE | PAGE_____ || ADDITIONAL CHILDREN | PAGE_____

_____ | _____

FATHER'S NAME | PAGE _____   MOTHER'S NAME | PAGE _____

NAME GIVEN AT BIRTH

_____   _____
DATE OF BIRTH   DATE OF DEATH

_____   _____
PLACE OF BIRTH   PLACE OF DEATH

_____
NAME OF SPOUSE | PAGE _____

_____   _____
MARITAL STATUS & DATE OF MARRIAGE   PLACE OF MARRIAGE

CHILDREN

_____   _____
NAME | PAGE _____   NAME | PAGE _____

_____   _____
NAME | PAGE _____   NAME | PAGE _____

_____   _____
NAME | PAGE _____   NAME | PAGE _____

_____   _____
NAME | PAGE _____   NAME | PAGE _____

_____   _____
NAME | PAGE _____   NAME | PAGE _____

NOTABLE CHARACTERISTICS & LIFE EVENTS: _____

_____

_____

_____

ADDITIONAL SPOUSE | PAGE_____ || ADDITIONAL CHILDREN | PAGE_____

FATHER'S NAME | PAGE _____

MOTHER'S NAME | PAGE _____

NAME GIVEN AT BIRTH

_____
DATE OF BIRTH

_____
DATE OF DEATH

_____
PLACE OF BIRTH

_____
PLACE OF DEATH

_____
NAME OF SPOUSE | PAGE _____

_____
MARITAL STATUS & DATE OF MARRIAGE

_____
PLACE OF MARRIAGE

CHILDREN

NAME | PAGE _____

NAME | PAGE _____

NAME | PAGE _____

NAME | PAGE _____

NAME | PAGE _____

NAME | PAGE _____

NAME | PAGE _____

NAME | PAGE _____

NAME | PAGE _____

NAME | PAGE _____

NOTABLE CHARACTERISTICS & LIFE EVENTS:

_____

_____

_____

ADDITIONAL SPOUSE | PAGE_____ || ADDITIONAL CHILDREN | PAGE_____

CHARTS INCLUDED IN | PAGE _____ || APPEARS IN PHOTOS | PAGE _____ || MENTIONED IN PAGES _____

_____ _____

FATHER'S NAME | PAGE _____   MOTHER'S NAME | PAGE _____

_____

NAME GIVEN AT BIRTH

_____   _____
DATE OF BIRTH   DATE OF DEATH

_____   _____
PLACE OF BIRTH   PLACE OF DEATH

_____
NAME OF SPOUSE | PAGE _____

_____   _____
MARITAL STATUS & DATE OF MARRIAGE   PLACE OF MARRIAGE

CHILDREN

_____   _____
NAME | PAGE _____   NAME | PAGE _____

_____   _____
NAME | PAGE _____   NAME | PAGE _____

_____   _____
NAME | PAGE _____   NAME | PAGE _____

_____   _____
NAME | PAGE _____   NAME | PAGE _____

_____   _____
NAME | PAGE _____   NAME | PAGE _____

NOTABLE CHARACTERISTICS & LIFE EVENTS: _____

_____

_____

_____

ADDITIONAL SPOUSE | PAGE _____ || ADDITIONAL CHILDREN | PAGE _____

CHARTS INCLUDED IN | PAGE _____ || APPEARS IN PHOTOS | PAGE _____ || MENTIONED IN PAGES _____

FATHER'S NAME | PAGE _____

MOTHER'S NAME | PAGE _____

NAME GIVEN AT BIRTH

_____
DATE OF BIRTH

_____
DATE OF DEATH

_____
PLACE OF BIRTH

_____
PLACE OF DEATH

_____
NAME OF SPOUSE | PAGE _____

_____
MARITAL STATUS & DATE OF MARRIAGE

_____
PLACE OF MARRIAGE

CHILDREN

_____
NAME | PAGE _____

_____
NAME | PAGE _____

_____
NAME | PAGE _____

_____
NAME | PAGE _____

_____
NAME | PAGE _____

_____
NAME | PAGE _____

_____
NAME | PAGE _____

_____
NAME | PAGE _____

_____
NAME | PAGE _____

_____
NAME | PAGE _____

NOTABLE CHARACTERISTICS & LIFE EVENTS:

ADDITIONAL SPOUSE | PAGE _____ || ADDITIONAL CHILDREN | PAGE _____

CHARTS INCLUDED IN | PAGE _____ || APPEARS IN PHOTOS | PAGE _____ || MENTIONED IN PAGES _____

FATHER'S NAME | PAGE _____

MOTHER'S NAME | PAGE _____

NAME GIVEN AT BIRTH

_____
DATE OF BIRTH

_____
PLACE OF BIRTH

_____
DATE OF DEATH

_____
PLACE OF DEATH

_____
NAME OF SPOUSE | PAGE_____

_____
MARITAL STATUS & DATE OF MARRIAGE

_____
PLACE OF MARRIAGE

CHILDREN

_____
NAME | PAGE _____

_____
NAME | PAGE _____

_____
NAME | PAGE _____

_____
NAME | PAGE _____

_____
NAME | PAGE _____

_____
NAME | PAGE _____

_____
NAME | PAGE _____

_____
NAME | PAGE _____

_____
NAME | PAGE _____

_____
NAME | PAGE _____

NOTABLE CHARACTERISTICS & LIFE EVENTS:

_____
_____
_____
_____

ADDITIONAL SPOUSE | PAGE_____ || ADDITIONAL CHILDREN | PAGE_____

_____

FATHER'S NAME | PAGE _____

_____

MOTHER'S NAME | PAGE _____

_____

NAME GIVEN AT BIRTH

_____

DATE OF BIRTH

_____

DATE OF DEATH

_____

PLACE OF BIRTH

_____

PLACE OF DEATH

_____

NAME OF SPOUSE | PAGE_____

_____

MARITAL STATUS & DATE OF MARRIAGE

_____

PLACE OF MARRIAGE

CHILDREN

_____

NAME | PAGE _____

_____

NAME | PAGE _____

_____

NAME | PAGE _____

_____

NAME | PAGE _____

_____

NAME | PAGE _____

_____

NAME | PAGE _____

_____

NAME | PAGE _____

_____

NAME | PAGE _____

_____

NAME | PAGE _____

_____

NAME | PAGE _____

NOTABLE CHARACTERISTICS & LIFE EVENTS:

_____

_____

_____

_____

ADDITIONAL SPOUSE | PAGE_____ || ADDITIONAL CHILDREN | PAGE_____

CHARTS INCLUDED IN | PAGE _____ || APPEARS IN PHOTOS | PAGE _____ || MENTIONED IN PAGES _____

_____ FATHER'S NAME | PAGE _____

_____ MOTHER'S NAME | PAGE _____

_____

NAME GIVEN AT BIRTH

_____
DATE OF BIRTH

_____
DATE OF DEATH

_____
PLACE OF BIRTH

_____
PLACE OF DEATH

_____
NAME OF SPOUSE | PAGE_____

_____
MARITAL STATUS & DATE OF MARRIAGE

_____
PLACE OF MARRIAGE

CHILDREN

_____
NAME | PAGE _____

_____
NAME | PAGE _____

_____
NAME | PAGE _____

_____
NAME | PAGE _____

_____
NAME | PAGE _____

_____
NAME | PAGE _____

_____
NAME | PAGE _____

_____
NAME | PAGE _____

_____
NAME | PAGE _____

_____
NAME | PAGE _____

NOTABLE CHARACTERISTICS & LIFE EVENTS: _____

_____

_____

_____

ADDITIONAL SPOUSE | PAGE_____ || ADDITIONAL CHILDREN | PAGE_____

_____

FATHER'S NAME | PAGE _____

_____

MOTHER'S NAME | PAGE _____

_____

NAME GIVEN AT BIRTH

_____
DATE OF BIRTH

_____
DATE OF DEATH

_____
PLACE OF BIRTH

_____
PLACE OF DEATH

_____
NAME OF SPOUSE | PAGE_____

_____
MARITAL STATUS & DATE OF MARRIAGE

_____
PLACE OF MARRIAGE

CHILDREN

_____
NAME | PAGE _____

_____
NAME | PAGE _____

_____
NAME | PAGE _____

_____
NAME | PAGE _____

_____
NAME | PAGE _____

_____
NAME | PAGE _____

_____
NAME | PAGE _____

_____
NAME | PAGE _____

_____
NAME | PAGE _____

_____
NAME | PAGE _____

NOTABLE CHARACTERISTICS & LIFE EVENTS: _____

_____

_____

_____

ADDITIONAL SPOUSE | PAGE_____ || ADDITIONAL CHILDREN | PAGE_____

CHARTS INCLUDED IN | PAGE _____ || APPEARS IN PHOTOS | PAGE _____ || MENTIONED IN PAGES _____

FATHER'S NAME | PAGE _____

MOTHER'S NAME | PAGE _____

NAME GIVEN AT BIRTH

_____
DATE OF BIRTH

_____
PLACE OF BIRTH

_____
DATE OF DEATH

_____
PLACE OF DEATH

_____
NAME OF SPOUSE | PAGE_____

_____
MARITAL STATUS & DATE OF MARRIAGE

_____
PLACE OF MARRIAGE

CHILDREN

_____
NAME | PAGE _____

_____
NAME | PAGE _____

_____
NAME | PAGE _____

_____
NAME | PAGE _____

_____
NAME | PAGE _____

_____
NAME | PAGE _____

_____
NAME | PAGE _____

_____
NAME | PAGE _____

_____
NAME | PAGE _____

_____
NAME | PAGE _____

NOTABLE CHARACTERISTICS & LIFE EVENTS: _____

_____

_____

_____

ADDITIONAL SPOUSE | PAGE_____ || ADDITIONAL CHILDREN | PAGE_____

_____
FATHER'S NAME | PAGE _____

_____
MOTHER'S NAME | PAGE _____

NAME GIVEN AT BIRTH

_____
DATE OF BIRTH

_____
DATE OF DEATH

_____
PLACE OF BIRTH

_____
PLACE OF DEATH

_____
NAME OF SPOUSE | PAGE _____

_____
MARITAL STATUS & DATE OF MARRIAGE

_____
PLACE OF MARRIAGE

CHILDREN

_____
NAME | PAGE _____

_____
NAME | PAGE _____

_____
NAME | PAGE _____

_____
NAME | PAGE _____

_____
NAME | PAGE _____

_____
NAME | PAGE _____

_____
NAME | PAGE _____

_____
NAME | PAGE _____

_____
NAME | PAGE _____

_____
NAME | PAGE _____

NOTABLE CHARACTERISTICS & LIFE EVENTS:

_____

_____

_____

_____

ADDITIONAL SPOUSE | PAGE _____ || ADDITIONAL CHILDREN | PAGE _____

_____

FATHER'S NAME | PAGE _____

_____

MOTHER'S NAME | PAGE _____

_____

NAME GIVEN AT BIRTH

_____

DATE OF BIRTH

_____

DATE OF DEATH

_____

PLACE OF BIRTH

_____

PLACE OF DEATH

_____

NAME OF SPOUSE | PAGE_____

_____

MARITAL STATUS & DATE OF MARRIAGE

_____

PLACE OF MARRIAGE

CHILDREN

_____

NAME | PAGE _____

_____

NAME | PAGE _____

_____

NAME | PAGE _____

_____

NAME | PAGE _____

_____

NAME | PAGE _____

_____

NAME | PAGE _____

_____

NAME | PAGE _____

_____

NAME | PAGE _____

_____

NAME | PAGE _____

_____

NAME | PAGE _____

NOTABLE CHARACTERISTICS & LIFE EVENTS:

_____

_____

_____

_____

ADDITIONAL SPOUSE | PAGE_____ || ADDITIONAL CHILDREN | PAGE_____

CHARTS INCLUDED IN | PAGE _____ || APPEARS IN PHOTOS | PAGE _____ || MENTIONED IN PAGES _____

FATHER'S NAME | PAGE _____

MOTHER'S NAME | PAGE _____

NAME GIVEN AT BIRTH

_____
DATE OF BIRTH

_____
PLACE OF BIRTH

_____
DATE OF DEATH

_____
PLACE OF DEATH

_____
NAME OF SPOUSE | PAGE _____

_____
MARITAL STATUS & DATE OF MARRIAGE

_____
PLACE OF MARRIAGE

CHILDREN

_____
NAME | PAGE _____

_____
NAME | PAGE _____

_____
NAME | PAGE _____

_____
NAME | PAGE _____

_____
NAME | PAGE _____

_____
NAME | PAGE _____

_____
NAME | PAGE _____

_____
NAME | PAGE _____

_____
NAME | PAGE _____

_____
NAME | PAGE _____

NOTABLE CHARACTERISTICS & LIFE EVENTS:

_____

_____

_____

_____

ADDITIONAL SPOUSE | PAGE_____ || ADDITIONAL CHILDREN | PAGE_____

CHARTS INCLUDED IN | PAGE _____ || APPEARS IN PHOTOS | PAGE _____ || MENTIONED IN PAGES _____

FATHER'S NAME | PAGE _____

MOTHER'S NAME | PAGE _____

NAME GIVEN AT BIRTH

_____
DATE OF BIRTH

_____
DATE OF DEATH

_____
PLACE OF BIRTH

_____
PLACE OF DEATH

NAME OF SPOUSE | PAGE _____

MARITAL STATUS & DATE OF MARRIAGE

PLACE OF MARRIAGE

CHILDREN

NAME | PAGE _____

NAME | PAGE _____

NAME | PAGE _____

NAME | PAGE _____

NAME | PAGE _____

NAME | PAGE _____

NAME | PAGE _____

NAME | PAGE _____

NAME | PAGE _____

NAME | PAGE _____

NOTABLE CHARACTERISTICS & LIFE EVENTS:

_____

_____

_____

_____

ADDITIONAL SPOUSE | PAGE _____ || ADDITIONAL CHILDREN | PAGE _____

CHARTS INCLUDED IN | PAGE _____ || APPEARS IN PHOTOS | PAGE _____ || MENTIONED IN PAGES _____

_____ _____

FATHER'S NAME | PAGE _____   MOTHER'S NAME | PAGE _____

NAME GIVEN AT BIRTH

_____   _____

DATE OF BIRTH   DATE OF DEATH

_____   _____

PLACE OF BIRTH   PLACE OF DEATH

_____

NAME OF SPOUSE | PAGE_____

_____   _____

MARITAL STATUS & DATE OF MARRIAGE   PLACE OF MARRIAGE

CHILDREN

_____   _____

NAME | PAGE _____   NAME | PAGE _____

_____   _____

NAME | PAGE _____   NAME | PAGE _____

_____   _____

NAME | PAGE _____   NAME | PAGE _____

_____   _____

NAME | PAGE _____   NAME | PAGE _____

_____   _____

NAME | PAGE _____   NAME | PAGE _____

NOTABLE CHARACTERISTICS & LIFE EVENTS: _____

_____

_____

_____

ADDITIONAL SPOUSE | PAGE_____ || ADDITIONAL CHILDREN | PAGE_____

_____

FATHER'S NAME | PAGE _____

_____

MOTHER'S NAME | PAGE _____

_____

NAME GIVEN AT BIRTH

_____
DATE OF BIRTH

_____
DATE OF DEATH

_____
PLACE OF BIRTH

_____
PLACE OF DEATH

_____
NAME OF SPOUSE | PAGE_____

_____
MARITAL STATUS & DATE OF MARRIAGE

_____
PLACE OF MARRIAGE

CHILDREN

_____
NAME | PAGE _____

_____
NAME | PAGE _____

_____
NAME | PAGE _____

_____
NAME | PAGE _____

_____
NAME | PAGE _____

_____
NAME | PAGE _____

_____
NAME | PAGE _____

_____
NAME | PAGE _____

_____
NAME | PAGE _____

_____
NAME | PAGE _____

NOTABLE CHARACTERISTICS & LIFE EVENTS: _____

_____

_____

_____

ADDITIONAL SPOUSE | PAGE_____ || ADDITIONAL CHILDREN | PAGE_____

CHARTS INCLUDED IN | PAGE _____ || APPEARS IN PHOTOS | PAGE _____ || MENTIONED IN PAGES _____

FATHER'S NAME | PAGE _____

MOTHER'S NAME | PAGE _____

NAME GIVEN AT BIRTH

_____
DATE OF BIRTH

_____
DATE OF DEATH

_____
PLACE OF BIRTH

_____
PLACE OF DEATH

_____
NAME OF SPOUSE | PAGE_____

_____
MARITAL STATUS & DATE OF MARRIAGE

_____
PLACE OF MARRIAGE

CHILDREN

_____
NAME | PAGE _____

_____
NAME | PAGE _____

_____
NAME | PAGE _____

_____
NAME | PAGE _____

_____
NAME | PAGE _____

_____
NAME | PAGE _____

_____
NAME | PAGE _____

_____
NAME | PAGE _____

_____
NAME | PAGE _____

_____
NAME | PAGE _____

NOTABLE CHARACTERISTICS & LIFE EVENTS: _____

_____

_____

_____

ADDITIONAL SPOUSE | PAGE_____ || ADDITIONAL CHILDREN | PAGE_____

_____ | _____
FATHER'S NAME | PAGE _____ | MOTHER'S NAME | PAGE _____

_____

NAME GIVEN AT BIRTH

_____
DATE OF BIRTH

_____
DATE OF DEATH

_____
PLACE OF BIRTH

_____
PLACE OF DEATH

_____
NAME OF SPOUSE | PAGE _____

_____
MARITAL STATUS & DATE OF MARRIAGE

_____
PLACE OF MARRIAGE

CHILDREN

_____
NAME | PAGE _____

_____
NAME | PAGE _____

_____
NAME | PAGE _____

_____
NAME | PAGE _____

_____
NAME | PAGE _____

_____
NAME | PAGE _____

_____
NAME | PAGE _____

_____
NAME | PAGE _____

_____
NAME | PAGE _____

_____
NAME | PAGE _____

NOTABLE CHARACTERISTICS & LIFE EVENTS:
_____
_____
_____
_____

ADDITIONAL SPOUSE | PAGE_____ || ADDITIONAL CHILDREN | PAGE_____

CHARTS INCLUDED IN | PAGE _____ || APPEARS IN PHOTOS | PAGE _____ || MENTIONED IN PAGES _____

_____

FATHER'S NAME | PAGE _____

_____

MOTHER'S NAME | PAGE _____

_____

NAME GIVEN AT BIRTH

_____
DATE OF BIRTH

_____
DATE OF DEATH

_____
PLACE OF BIRTH

_____
PLACE OF DEATH

_____
NAME OF SPOUSE | PAGE_____

_____
MARITAL STATUS & DATE OF MARRIAGE

_____
PLACE OF MARRIAGE

CHILDREN

_____
NAME | PAGE _____

_____
NAME | PAGE _____

_____
NAME | PAGE _____

_____
NAME | PAGE _____

_____
NAME | PAGE _____

_____
NAME | PAGE _____

_____
NAME | PAGE _____

_____
NAME | PAGE _____

_____
NAME | PAGE _____

_____
NAME | PAGE _____

NOTABLE CHARACTERISTICS & LIFE EVENTS: _____

_____

_____

_____

ADDITIONAL SPOUSE | PAGE_____ || ADDITIONAL CHILDREN | PAGE_____

CHARTS INCLUDED IN | PAGE _____ || APPEARS IN PHOTOS | PAGE _____ || MENTIONED IN PAGES _____

_____

FATHER'S NAME | PAGE _____

_____

MOTHER'S NAME | PAGE _____

_____

NAME GIVEN AT BIRTH

_____

DATE OF BIRTH

_____

DATE OF DEATH

_____

PLACE OF BIRTH

_____

PLACE OF DEATH

_____

NAME OF SPOUSE | PAGE_____

_____   _____

MARITAL STATUS & DATE OF MARRIAGE   PLACE OF MARRIAGE

CHILDREN

_____   _____

NAME | PAGE _____   NAME | PAGE _____

_____   _____

NAME | PAGE _____   NAME | PAGE _____

_____   _____

NAME | PAGE _____   NAME | PAGE _____

_____   _____

NAME | PAGE _____   NAME | PAGE _____

_____   _____

NAME | PAGE _____   NAME | PAGE _____

NOTABLE CHARACTERISTICS & LIFE EVENTS: _____

_____

_____

_____

ADDITIONAL SPOUSE | PAGE_____ || ADDITIONAL CHILDREN | PAGE_____

_____

FATHER'S NAME | PAGE _____   MOTHER'S NAME | PAGE _____

_____

NAME GIVEN AT BIRTH

_____   _____

DATE OF BIRTH   DATE OF DEATH

_____   _____

PLACE OF BIRTH   PLACE OF DEATH

_____

NAME OF SPOUSE | PAGE_____

_____   _____

MARITAL STATUS & DATE OF MARRIAGE   PLACE OF MARRIAGE

CHILDREN

_____   _____
NAME | PAGE _____   NAME | PAGE _____

_____   _____
NAME | PAGE _____   NAME | PAGE _____

_____   _____
NAME | PAGE _____   NAME | PAGE _____

_____   _____
NAME | PAGE _____   NAME | PAGE _____

_____   _____
NAME | PAGE _____   NAME | PAGE _____

NOTABLE CHARACTERISTICS & LIFE EVENTS: _____

_____

_____

_____

ADDITIONAL SPOUSE | PAGE_____ || ADDITIONAL CHILDREN | PAGE_____

_____

FATHER'S NAME | PAGE _____

_____

MOTHER'S NAME | PAGE _____

_____

NAME GIVEN AT BIRTH

_____

DATE OF BIRTH

_____

DATE OF DEATH

_____

PLACE OF BIRTH

_____

PLACE OF DEATH

_____

NAME OF SPOUSE | PAGE_____

_____

MARITAL STATUS & DATE OF MARRIAGE

_____

PLACE OF MARRIAGE

CHILDREN

_____

NAME | PAGE _____

_____

NAME | PAGE _____

_____

NAME | PAGE _____

_____

NAME | PAGE _____

_____

NAME | PAGE _____

_____

NAME | PAGE _____

_____

NAME | PAGE _____

_____

NAME | PAGE _____

_____

NAME | PAGE _____

_____

NAME | PAGE _____

NOTABLE CHARACTERISTICS & LIFE EVENTS:

_____

_____

_____

_____

ADDITIONAL SPOUSE | PAGE_____ || ADDITIONAL CHILDREN | PAGE_____

CHARTS INCLUDED IN | PAGE _____ || APPEARS IN PHOTOS | PAGE _____ || MENTIONED IN PAGES _____

FATHER'S NAME | PAGE _____

MOTHER'S NAME | PAGE _____

NAME GIVEN AT BIRTH

_____
DATE OF BIRTH

_____
PLACE OF BIRTH

_____
DATE OF DEATH

_____
PLACE OF DEATH

_____
NAME OF SPOUSE | PAGE _____

_____
MARITAL STATUS & DATE OF MARRIAGE

_____
PLACE OF MARRIAGE

CHILDREN

_____
NAME | PAGE _____

_____
NAME | PAGE _____

_____
NAME | PAGE _____

_____
NAME | PAGE _____

_____
NAME | PAGE _____

_____
NAME | PAGE _____

_____
NAME | PAGE _____

_____
NAME | PAGE _____

_____
NAME | PAGE _____

_____
NAME | PAGE _____

NOTABLE CHARACTERISTICS & LIFE EVENTS: _____

_____

_____

_____

ADDITIONAL SPOUSE | PAGE _____ || ADDITIONAL CHILDREN | PAGE _____

FATHER'S NAME | PAGE _____

MOTHER'S NAME | PAGE _____

NAME GIVEN AT BIRTH

_____
DATE OF BIRTH

_____
DATE OF DEATH

_____
PLACE OF BIRTH

_____
PLACE OF DEATH

_____
NAME OF SPOUSE | PAGE _____

_____
MARITAL STATUS & DATE OF MARRIAGE

_____
PLACE OF MARRIAGE

CHILDREN

_____
NAME | PAGE _____

_____
NAME | PAGE _____

_____
NAME | PAGE _____

_____
NAME | PAGE _____

_____
NAME | PAGE _____

_____
NAME | PAGE _____

_____
NAME | PAGE _____

_____
NAME | PAGE _____

_____
NAME | PAGE _____

_____
NAME | PAGE _____

NOTABLE CHARACTERISTICS & LIFE EVENTS:

_____

_____

_____

_____

ADDITIONAL SPOUSE | PAGE_____ || ADDITIONAL CHILDREN | PAGE_____

FATHER'S NAME | PAGE _____

MOTHER'S NAME | PAGE _____

NAME GIVEN AT BIRTH

_____
DATE OF BIRTH

_____
DATE OF DEATH

_____
PLACE OF BIRTH

_____
PLACE OF DEATH

_____
NAME OF SPOUSE | PAGE _____

_____
MARITAL STATUS & DATE OF MARRIAGE

_____
PLACE OF MARRIAGE

CHILDREN

_____
NAME | PAGE _____

_____
NAME | PAGE _____

_____
NAME | PAGE _____

_____
NAME | PAGE _____

_____
NAME | PAGE _____

_____
NAME | PAGE _____

_____
NAME | PAGE _____

_____
NAME | PAGE _____

_____
NAME | PAGE _____

_____
NAME | PAGE _____

NOTABLE CHARACTERISTICS & LIFE EVENTS: _____

_____

_____

_____

ADDITIONAL SPOUSE | PAGE _____ || ADDITIONAL CHILDREN | PAGE _____

_____

FATHER'S NAME | PAGE _____

_____

MOTHER'S NAME | PAGE _____

_____

NAME GIVEN AT BIRTH

_____

DATE OF BIRTH

_____

DATE OF DEATH

_____

PLACE OF BIRTH

_____

PLACE OF DEATH

_____

NAME OF SPOUSE | PAGE _____

_____

MARITAL STATUS & DATE OF MARRIAGE

_____

PLACE OF MARRIAGE

CHILDREN

_____

NAME | PAGE _____

_____

NAME | PAGE _____

_____

NAME | PAGE _____

_____

NAME | PAGE _____

_____

NAME | PAGE _____

_____

NAME | PAGE _____

_____

NAME | PAGE _____

_____

NAME | PAGE _____

_____

NAME | PAGE _____

_____

NAME | PAGE _____

NOTABLE CHARACTERISTICS & LIFE EVENTS: _____

_____

_____

_____

ADDITIONAL SPOUSE | PAGE _____ || ADDITIONAL CHILDREN | PAGE _____

CHARTS INCLUDED IN | PAGE _____ || APPEARS IN PHOTOS | PAGE _____ || MENTIONED IN PAGES _____

_____

FATHER'S NAME | PAGE _____

_____

MOTHER'S NAME | PAGE _____

_____

NAME GIVEN AT BIRTH

_____

DATE OF BIRTH

_____

DATE OF DEATH

_____

PLACE OF BIRTH

_____

PLACE OF DEATH

_____

NAME OF SPOUSE | PAGE_____

_____

MARITAL STATUS & DATE OF MARRIAGE

_____

PLACE OF MARRIAGE

CHILDREN

_____

NAME | PAGE _____

_____

NAME | PAGE _____

_____

NAME | PAGE _____

_____

NAME | PAGE _____

_____

NAME | PAGE _____

_____

NAME | PAGE _____

_____

NAME | PAGE _____

_____

NAME | PAGE _____

_____

NAME | PAGE _____

_____

NAME | PAGE _____

NOTABLE CHARACTERISTICS & LIFE EVENTS:

_____

_____

_____

_____

ADDITIONAL SPOUSE | PAGE_____ || ADDITIONAL CHILDREN | PAGE_____

_____ _____

FATHER'S NAME | PAGE _____   MOTHER'S NAME | PAGE _____

_____

NAME GIVEN AT BIRTH

_____   _____

DATE OF BIRTH   DATE OF DEATH

_____   _____

PLACE OF BIRTH   PLACE OF DEATH

_____

NAME OF SPOUSE | PAGE_____

_____   _____

MARITAL STATUS & DATE OF MARRIAGE   PLACE OF MARRIAGE

CHILDREN

_____   _____

NAME | PAGE _____   NAME | PAGE _____

_____   _____

NAME | PAGE _____   NAME | PAGE _____

_____   _____

NAME | PAGE _____   NAME | PAGE _____

_____   _____

NAME | PAGE _____   NAME | PAGE _____

_____   _____

NAME | PAGE _____   NAME | PAGE _____

NOTABLE CHARACTERISTICS & LIFE EVENTS: _____

_____

_____

_____

_____

ADDITIONAL SPOUSE | PAGE_____ || ADDITIONAL CHILDREN | PAGE_____

CHARTS INCLUDED IN | PAGE _____ || APPEARS IN PHOTOS | PAGE _____ || MENTIONED IN PAGES _____

FATHER'S NAME | PAGE _____

MOTHER'S NAME | PAGE _____

NAME GIVEN AT BIRTH

_____
DATE OF BIRTH

_____
PLACE OF BIRTH

_____
DATE OF DEATH

_____
PLACE OF DEATH

_____
NAME OF SPOUSE | PAGE _____

_____
MARITAL STATUS & DATE OF MARRIAGE

_____
PLACE OF MARRIAGE

CHILDREN

_____
NAME | PAGE _____

_____
NAME | PAGE _____

_____
NAME | PAGE _____

_____
NAME | PAGE _____

_____
NAME | PAGE _____

_____
NAME | PAGE _____

_____
NAME | PAGE _____

_____
NAME | PAGE _____

_____
NAME | PAGE _____

_____
NAME | PAGE _____

NOTABLE CHARACTERISTICS & LIFE EVENTS: _____

_____

_____

_____

ADDITIONAL SPOUSE | PAGE _____ || ADDITIONAL CHILDREN | PAGE _____

CHARTS INCLUDED IN | PAGE _____ || APPEARS IN PHOTOS | PAGE _____ || MENTIONED IN PAGES _____

_____

FATHER'S NAME | PAGE _____

_____

MOTHER'S NAME | PAGE _____

_____

NAME GIVEN AT BIRTH

_____

DATE OF BIRTH

_____

DATE OF DEATH

_____

PLACE OF BIRTH

_____

PLACE OF DEATH

_____

NAME OF SPOUSE | PAGE_____

_____

MARITAL STATUS & DATE OF MARRIAGE

_____

PLACE OF MARRIAGE

CHILDREN

_____

NAME | PAGE _____

_____

NAME | PAGE _____

_____

NAME | PAGE _____

_____

NAME | PAGE _____

_____

NAME | PAGE _____

_____

NAME | PAGE _____

_____

NAME | PAGE _____

_____

NAME | PAGE _____

_____

NAME | PAGE _____

_____

NAME | PAGE _____

NOTABLE CHARACTERISTICS & LIFE EVENTS:

_____

_____

_____

_____

ADDITIONAL SPOUSE | PAGE_____ || ADDITIONAL CHILDREN | PAGE_____

CHARTS INCLUDED IN | PAGE _____ || APPEARS IN PHOTOS | PAGE _____ || MENTIONED IN PAGES _____

FATHER'S NAME | PAGE _____

MOTHER'S NAME | PAGE _____

NAME GIVEN AT BIRTH

_____
DATE OF BIRTH

_____
DATE OF DEATH

_____
PLACE OF BIRTH

_____
PLACE OF DEATH

_____
NAME OF SPOUSE | PAGE_____

_____
MARITAL STATUS & DATE OF MARRIAGE

_____
PLACE OF MARRIAGE

CHILDREN

NAME | PAGE _____	NAME | PAGE _____
NAME | PAGE _____	NAME | PAGE _____
NAME | PAGE _____	NAME | PAGE _____
NAME | PAGE _____	NAME | PAGE _____
NAME | PAGE _____	NAME | PAGE _____

NOTABLE CHARACTERISTICS & LIFE EVENTS:

_____

_____

_____

_____

ADDITIONAL SPOUSE | PAGE_____ || ADDITIONAL CHILDREN | PAGE_____

FATHER'S NAME | PAGE _____

MOTHER'S NAME | PAGE _____

NAME GIVEN AT BIRTH

_____
DATE OF BIRTH

_____
DATE OF DEATH

_____
PLACE OF BIRTH

_____
PLACE OF DEATH

NAME OF SPOUSE | PAGE_____

_____
MARITAL STATUS & DATE OF MARRIAGE

_____
PLACE OF MARRIAGE

CHILDREN

_____
NAME | PAGE _____

_____
NAME | PAGE _____

_____
NAME | PAGE _____

_____
NAME | PAGE _____

_____
NAME | PAGE _____

_____
NAME | PAGE _____

_____
NAME | PAGE _____

_____
NAME | PAGE _____

_____
NAME | PAGE _____

_____
NAME | PAGE _____

NOTABLE CHARACTERISTICS & LIFE EVENTS:

_____

_____

_____

ADDITIONAL SPOUSE | PAGE_____ || ADDITIONAL CHILDREN | PAGE_____

CHARTS INCLUDED IN | PAGE _____ || APPEARS IN PHOTOS | PAGE _____ || MENTIONED IN PAGES _____

_____

FATHER'S NAME | PAGE _____

_____

MOTHER'S NAME | PAGE _____

_____

NAME GIVEN AT BIRTH

_____

DATE OF BIRTH

_____

DATE OF DEATH

_____

PLACE OF BIRTH

_____

PLACE OF DEATH

_____

NAME OF SPOUSE | PAGE_____

_____

MARITAL STATUS & DATE OF MARRIAGE

_____

PLACE OF MARRIAGE

CHILDREN

_____

NAME | PAGE _____

_____

NAME | PAGE _____

_____

NAME | PAGE _____

_____

NAME | PAGE _____

_____

NAME | PAGE _____

_____

NAME | PAGE _____

_____

NAME | PAGE _____

_____

NAME | PAGE _____

_____

NAME | PAGE _____

_____

NAME | PAGE _____

NOTABLE CHARACTERISTICS & LIFE EVENTS:

_____

_____

_____

_____

ADDITIONAL SPOUSE | PAGE_____ || ADDITIONAL CHILDREN | PAGE_____

_____ _____

FATHER'S NAME | PAGE _____   MOTHER'S NAME | PAGE _____

_____

NAME GIVEN AT BIRTH

_____   _____

DATE OF BIRTH   DATE OF DEATH

_____   _____

PLACE OF BIRTH   PLACE OF DEATH

_____

NAME OF SPOUSE | PAGE_____

_____   _____

MARITAL STATUS & DATE OF MARRIAGE   PLACE OF MARRIAGE

CHILDREN

_____   _____

NAME | PAGE _____   NAME | PAGE _____

_____   _____

NAME | PAGE _____   NAME | PAGE _____

_____   _____

NAME | PAGE _____   NAME | PAGE _____

_____   _____

NAME | PAGE _____   NAME | PAGE _____

_____   _____

NAME | PAGE _____   NAME | PAGE _____

NOTABLE CHARACTERISTICS & LIFE EVENTS: _____

_____

_____

_____

ADDITIONAL SPOUSE | PAGE_____ || ADDITIONAL CHILDREN | PAGE_____

CHARTS INCLUDED IN | PAGE _____ || APPEARS IN PHOTOS | PAGE _____ || MENTIONED IN PAGES _____

FATHER'S NAME | PAGE _____

MOTHER'S NAME | PAGE _____

NAME GIVEN AT BIRTH

_____
DATE OF BIRTH

_____
PLACE OF BIRTH

_____
DATE OF DEATH

_____
PLACE OF DEATH

_____
NAME OF SPOUSE | PAGE _____

_____
MARITAL STATUS & DATE OF MARRIAGE

_____
PLACE OF MARRIAGE

CHILDREN

NAME | PAGE _____

NAME | PAGE _____

NAME | PAGE _____

NAME | PAGE _____

NAME | PAGE _____

NAME | PAGE _____

NAME | PAGE _____

NAME | PAGE _____

NAME | PAGE _____

NAME | PAGE _____

NOTABLE CHARACTERISTICS & LIFE EVENTS:

_____

_____

_____

_____

ADDITIONAL SPOUSE | PAGE_____ || ADDITIONAL CHILDREN | PAGE_____

FATHER'S NAME | PAGE _____

MOTHER'S NAME | PAGE _____

NAME GIVEN AT BIRTH

_____
DATE OF BIRTH

_____
DATE OF DEATH

_____
PLACE OF BIRTH

_____
PLACE OF DEATH

_____
NAME OF SPOUSE | PAGE_____

_____
MARITAL STATUS & DATE OF MARRIAGE

_____
PLACE OF MARRIAGE

CHILDREN

_____
NAME | PAGE _____

_____
NAME | PAGE _____

_____
NAME | PAGE _____

_____
NAME | PAGE _____

_____
NAME | PAGE _____

_____
NAME | PAGE _____

_____
NAME | PAGE _____

_____
NAME | PAGE _____

_____
NAME | PAGE _____

_____
NAME | PAGE _____

NOTABLE CHARACTERISTICS & LIFE EVENTS: _____

_____

_____

_____

ADDITIONAL SPOUSE | PAGE_____ || ADDITIONAL CHILDREN | PAGE_____

FATHER'S NAME | PAGE _____

MOTHER'S NAME | PAGE _____

NAME GIVEN AT BIRTH

_____
DATE OF BIRTH

_____
DATE OF DEATH

_____
PLACE OF BIRTH

_____
PLACE OF DEATH

_____
NAME OF SPOUSE | PAGE_____

_____
MARITAL STATUS & DATE OF MARRIAGE

_____
PLACE OF MARRIAGE

CHILDREN

_____
NAME | PAGE _____

_____
NAME | PAGE _____

_____
NAME | PAGE _____

_____
NAME | PAGE _____

_____
NAME | PAGE _____

_____
NAME | PAGE _____

_____
NAME | PAGE _____

_____
NAME | PAGE _____

_____
NAME | PAGE _____

_____
NAME | PAGE _____

NOTABLE CHARACTERISTICS & LIFE EVENTS:

_____

_____

_____

_____

INDEX OF FAMILY MEMBERS

NAME:

	PAGE
	PAGE
	PAGE
	PAGE
	PAGE
	PAGE
	PAGE
	PAGE
	PAGE
	PAGE
	PAGE
	PAGE
	PAGE
	PAGE
	PAGE
	PAGE
	PAGE
	PAGE
	PAGE
	PAGE
	PAGE
	PAGE
	PAGE
	PAGE

NAME:

	PAGE
	PAGE
	PAGE
	PAGE
	PAGE
	PAGE
	PAGE
	PAGE
	PAGE
	PAGE
	PAGE
	PAGE
	PAGE
	PAGE
	PAGE
	PAGE
	PAGE
	PAGE
	PAGE
	PAGE
	PAGE
	PAGE
	PAGE
	PAGE

INDEX OF FAMILY MEMBERS

NAME:

	PAGE
	PAGE
	PAGE
	PAGE
	PAGE
	PAGE
	PAGE
	PAGE
	PAGE
	PAGE
	PAGE
	PAGE
	PAGE
	PAGE
	PAGE
	PAGE
	PAGE
	PAGE
	PAGE
	PAGE
	PAGE
	PAGE
	PAGE
	PAGE
	PAGE

NAME:

	PAGE
	PAGE
	PAGE
	PAGE
	PAGE
	PAGE
	PAGE
	PAGE
	PAGE
	PAGE
	PAGE
	PAGE
	PAGE
	PAGE
	PAGE
	PAGE
	PAGE
	PAGE
	PAGE
	PAGE
	PAGE
	PAGE
	PAGE
	PAGE
	PAGE

NOTES

NOTES

SURNAMES INCLUDED IN THIS BOOK

Made in the USA
Las Vegas, NV
07 November 2024

11303806R00083